SELF-LOVE FOR TEEN GIRLS

9 Steps to Transform Your
Mindset, Build Self-Esteem, and
Create a Life You Truly Love

The Mentor Bucket

Table of Contents

INTRODUCTION

Hey there!

Take a few moments to look in the mirror and say to yourself, *"I love myself just the way I am!"*

Yes, you need to say that out loud to yourself often because regardless of how you see yourself, you are worthy of being loved, and you need to love yourself for **YOU!**

Many years ago, I wished I could say the same, but I couldn't say anything close to that because I never loved myself. Well, I didn't see anything lovable about me.

Looking back now, I can see that I've come a long way on my journey to achieving limitless self-love. I could say those words I dreaded so much repeatedly without thinking much about it. And you know what's even better? I am not just saying those words; I actually *believe* them.

I will not stand here and tell you that the journey to achieving self-love was easy; I'd be lying to you. Despite not being easy, it is attainable, and this book promises to be your guide every step of the way.

As a teen, it's very easy to get lost in how fast life is playing out, especially in high school when things happen fast. In your junior or senior year, you can feel like everything is thrown at you all at once, like an avalanche out of nowhere. When your SATs and college stuff come into the picture, you can get overwhelmed, and your emotions start running wild.

For me, the toughest times in my teenage years were my junior year and senior year. Before then, I remember being a healthy and happy child; I was eating healthily and was generally happy. Everyone knew me as an energetic and bubbly person. However, my life went through the biggest funk I ever experienced during my junior year.

I couldn't figure out why, but every day seemed awful; I was mostly sad. The constant sadness made me hate how I looked and hate doing the things I formerly loved, and I started avoiding people. There was nothing about me I liked anymore, and it started affecting all aspects of my life. I did a good job of hiding my emotions, but my close friends and family noticed. They knew I was no longer my happy self. I started ditching classes and binge eating because I was always feeling stressed.

I thought I was a failure in school, a loser in life, no one wanted to hang out with me, and something was wrong with me. These negative assumptions hurt my self-esteem, and I couldn't see anything good about myself. Everyone around me seemed happy, but I couldn't relate; I was too sad.

Now that I've scaled through and passed that stage, I understand that the voices in my head played a big role in how my teenage years turned out. Sometimes, these voices can be based on harsh words from others or bad situations you've faced. But you can change these voices and learn to think of yourself in better ways.

Perhaps, you want to feel confident about who you are. You're hoping that as you become a teenager, you'll see yourself in a better light—have all the confidence you've dreamed of and have a strong and positive mindset to unlock many possibilities, set up your life in ways you love, and achieve your goals.

However, your dreams are becoming far out of reach; they seem impossible as the days pass, and you wonder if your life will continue this way. The truth is, the teenage years are full of change. There's a "reorganization" that your brain experiences, and this makes you feel confused, overwhelmed, and exhausted. As you search for your place in the world, you'll start struggling with situations that challenge your beliefs about yourself.

As a result, you tend to avoid situations that might carry a risk of failure, bad decisions, or mistakes that could cause great embarrassment. These can involve situations in school, friendships, and trying out new things. But how long should you avoid these things, which are all essential to form a healthy teenage life?

When these issues become disturbing and nothing is done about them, they can lead to further problems such as low motivation, difficulty making friends, poor body image, early sexual activity, drug and alcohol use, and negative moods such as anger, sadness, anxiety, and shame.

Thankfully, you're reading this book, which will serve as your little pick-me-up for self-love, and life will only get better from here!

There will always be someone prettier than you, smarter than you, richer than you, luckier than you, and the list goes on and on. But that's how life is; humans are unique in their own form and experiences. So pipe down when next you catch yourself being unnecessarily harsh on yourself. Knowing that certain things are out of your control doesn't mean you're less human.

To me, self-love is what you should aim for. It's what makes you stand out from the crowd. It gives you an exquisite, radiant personality that illuminates from within you. When you've attained limitless self-love, you will know that no human is just like another. We all have unique features or personalities that make us all beautiful.

Self-love for teens is important as it allows you to see things differently, have healthy self-esteem, and brim with the confidence to go for anything you want. You'll be willing to try new things, solve problems, and take healthy risks. Your growth will be productive, setting you up for a positive future and a life you love.

I wish I had the kind of helpful information you're about to read. I wouldn't have needed to learn about self-love the hard way or go through a tough route to get to where I am today. Thankfully, you're reading a life-changing book that will, in no time, transform your mindset, build your self-esteem, and create the life you love.

The people in your life can affect how you feel about yourself. When you focus on what's good about you, you will feel good about yourself. If you're patient when you make mistakes, you'll learn to accept yourself. When you have friends and get along with them, you will feel loved by them.

But when the reverse is the case and adults scold you more than they praise you, it becomes hard to see anything good about yourself. Mean teasing by peers, bullying, and hurtful words from parents can stick with you and hurt your self-esteem. They can become part of how you see yourself. However, it doesn't have to be that way; you can change your life by learning to love yourself regardless of how others see you.

After reading this book, you're more likely to display positive behavioral characteristics such as trying out new things, learning from your failures (if there are any), acting more independently and maturely, helping others when you can, taking pride in your achievements or accomplishments, gaining more control over your emotions, silencing naysayers that discourage you from going after your dreams, and dealing with frustrations more responsibly.

This book will help put you at the center of your world. You'll gain access to nine distinct steps needed on your journey toward achieving self-love. The steps aim to change your beliefs and realize that you have inherent value and are worthy of being loved for who you are. You will find strategies for self-discovery, silencing the inner voices distracting you, and more.

By developing self-love, you support your inner strength so you can learn from your failures and excel in life. The younger you are when you start, the better. You can live the life of your dreams by loving yourself completely and gaining control over your mind and life.

Remember, the only hindrance to your best life is you; only you can take charge and change it! Are you ready to discover how to change your attitude, build confidence in who you are, and genuinely love yourself completely?

Let's get started!

Step One
Go on a Self-Discovery Journey

The teenage years are a critical time for you to learn your self-identity and get a healthy start in life. It is normal to go through developmental stages and identity exploration in your adolescent years. In conjunction with physiological and developmental changes happening in the brain and body, a journey of self-discovery is common for most teenagers.

Every teen seeks to discover their identity and place in the world. As a teenager, you can become a better version of yourself by adopting certain mindsets and participating in specific activities. To do this, you need to understand the physiological composition of your brain between the ages of 12 and 18.

The frontal lobe plays a vital role in the chemical makeup of a teenage brain. It's the part of your brain that says: *Should I do this? Is it a good idea? What would be the consequences if I did this?* Your frontal lobe develops throughout your adolescence and reaches maturity in adulthood.

This is why, unlike adults, teens struggle to understand or find their place in the world. It is the scientific reasoning for the selfish behavior most teens exhibit. Being a teenager means you don't always see outside of yourself. Still, there are subtle differences in character in adolescents ages 12 to 14 and ages 15 to 18.

This chapter will focus on self-discovery as a teen. You should be able to understand your identity, know your identity crisis, and learn strategies to help you start your self-discovery journey.

Understanding Your Identity

Not all teens experience an identity crisis. It is more prevalent among teens who were adopted or displaced, had a traumatic childhood, or struggled with mental health conditions. Certain family, cultural, and traditional factors and social expectations may also contribute to developing an identity crisis as you try to figure out who you are.

It's safe to assume that everyone struggles with their identity at some point. Even if you see adults who seem to know exactly who they are, they've probably experienced a few transitional periods.

Personally, my identity has evolved in conjunction with major life changes. How I defined myself as a teen significantly differs from how I define myself now. When I was in college as an eighteen-year-old, I tied my sense of identity to my college major. It made up a substantial part of who I was, and I couldn't introduce myself to people without attaching my major. Eventually, I resolved to make a decision about my identity after marriage.

Before we can understand what an identity crisis is, we must first understand what identity means. The concept of identity is tricky. At its core, it is subjective. Plus, the fact that we define our identity ourselves makes it even more complex.

Identity encompasses experiences, memories, values, and relationships. These are the components that create your identity and sense of self. As social beings, humans have learned to identify themselves in different ways.

We identify ourselves in certain ways to give others a shortcut to understanding who we are. This is why some people tie their identities to their careers, whereas others tie them to their relationships, families, or parenthood. Some also tie their identities to their hobbies, passions, and dreams.

Identity serves many purposes that contribute to happy and healthy living. Having a sense of identity is fundamental to having a sense of belonging. Finding communities and places where you belong is easier if you know exactly how to define yourself.

Your identity is a way to structure certain parts of your life and your choices to make them manageable. If your identity includes being outdoors, seeking experiences involving outdoor adventures is easier. You do this to reinforce your identity. But as helpful as this may be, you should know it can be limiting.

Identity plays a key role in social connections and emotional and mental well-being. We often tie identity to communities such as shared language, social or political values, religions, cultural experiences, etc.

Identity Crisis – All You Need to Know About Identity Crisis

Now that you know what identity is, what is an identity crisis?

An identity crisis is a developmental phase that involves questioning your sense of self or place. It happens any time a major change makes you reevaluate who you are. Developmental psychologist Erik Erikson introduced us to the concept of identity crisis via his work. He believed that identity formation is one of the biggest conflicts most people face in their lifetime.

Erikson observed that developing one's sense of identity during the teenage years is important. However, the growth and development of identity aren't limited to teenagehood. Instead, our identity changes as we face new challenges and gain new experiences. Thus, you can experience an identity crisis at any point in life, from adolescence to adulthood.

Erikson described an identity crisis as *"a time of intensive analysis and exploration of different ways of looking at oneself."* As I said, your identity is defined by your relationships, experiences, memories, beliefs, and values—all of which make up your sense of self. This creates a fairly constant self-image even as you develop and strengthen new aspects of yourself over time.

Figuring out your identity involves answering questions such as:

- *What are my passions?*
- *What are my beliefs?*
- *What are my values?*
- *What is my purpose in life?*
- *What is my role in family and society?*
- *Who am I? (regarding career, age, or relationship)?*

"Who am I?" is a question many teenagers ask, either internally or openly, depending on their personality and upbringing. When you ask this question for the first time, it is because you are starting to appreciate the significance of having your own identity.

Adolescence is a time when we experience major changes—physical, physiological, psychological, spiritual, psychosocial, etc. It is a critical transitional period; therefore, you are susceptible to an identity crisis at this stage.

Your teenage years are when you go through big changes and stress, which is why the above questions start to pop up in your mind. This can make you unmotivated and irritable. At the same time, you are intrinsically motivated to discover who you are. So, you invest lots of time and energy into pursuing identity discovery and formation.

You may use abstract thinking to visualize how others perceive you when you make certain changes, such as how you look. According to Erikson, the identity formation processes are highly cognitive and social.

Teenagers continually take cues from their environment and the people around them before making decisions or taking action. The opinions and reactions of family, friends, and, most importantly, peers play a vital role in forming your sense of who you are.

The process is pretty intense during your adolescent years, but the intensity will wane eventually. And the process will continue well into the future.

When I was 12 or 13 years of age, like other teens, I believed I knew everything there was to know about myself, my environment, the world, and life. I even took an online personality test that convinced me I knew myself as deeply as possible. I thought I had attained a level of self-awareness beyond other teenagers.

Interestingly, I took this test multiple times and got different results each time because I couldn't answer questions about myself accurately. Yet, I believed in my newly discovered self-awareness and relished what it implied—that I was smarter and more intelligent than any other kid my age. After all, how many of them had a sense of self-awareness like me?

Looking back, I realize now that I wasn't quite the smartypants I thought I was. Now I recognize that, like most teenagers, I had to embark on a quest for self-awareness—a desire to learn much about myself and how I fit in with my environment and the world. It was a journey of self-discovery, but I hadn't gone about it the right way.

Between 12 and 14, you might consider yourself more knowledgeable than the adults around you, constantly questioning everything in your environment and wanting to showcase your knowledge. Between ages 15 and 18, you become more idealistic, wanting to synthesize your ideas and express your feelings.

Based on this, it is obvious that your teenage years are a transformative period of growth for you. You may not be an adult yet, due to the physiological composition of your teenage brain. Yet, you want to grow up and emulate adult behavior.

Considering the distinction between your teenage brain and the adult brain, how do you best embark on a journey of self-discovery?

Self-discovery is a never-ending process that goes on throughout life. Still, awareness heightens the most during the teenage years. Your teenage years are the best time to start seeking answers to questions about who you are and the why and wherefore of your identity.

The desire to discover your identity is innate and ingrained in your brain. Unfortunately, this doesn't make the journey easier. The process of self-discovery is typically complicated by many factors and issues, which can make your journey arduous.

This puts you at risk of having an identity crisis. Core adolescent issues relating to independence can complicate self-discovery and identity formation. You can also experience other issues that may make the journey more complex than you can handle.

Not only can these issues intensify your struggle and impair the quality of your teen life, but they can also make you predisposed to emotional challenges and mental health problems. "Failing" in this identity formation and self-discovery task can impact not just your teenage years but also your adult years.

In your teen years, you are neither an adult nor a child. Going into adulthood can be one of the hardest roads you'll ever walk. It is normal if you feel the pull to want to hang on to your parents, as that is the child in you. At the same time, you will feel the pull to want to find your own way. This inner struggle is a burden you must bear, and it may be complicated by parents who don't want to let you go.

The search for your identity is a core part of the process, but not every teen has it easy. You could struggle as you adjust to different changes. The self-discovery and identity formation process is critical as it helps you understand the changes.

However, with these challenges, you may be unable to move forward successfully. An identity crisis may complicate this phase.

Remember that identity crises do not happen only during the teenage years. You can have an identity crisis whenever you experience a major life transition or find yourself in a significantly different role.

Figuring Out Your Identity Crisis

When you are undergoing an identity crisis, your life may seem somewhat chaotic. Since you are on a journey to discover who you are or who you will be as an adult, you may explore different roles in your relationships and behaviors.

Your beliefs and values begin to change and conflict with your old values as you enter a new phase of life and form a new sense of self. Along the way, it's normal to experience some uncertainty about who you are and where your place is in society.

The inability to move past this phase means your identity crisis will continue, leading to identity confusion. However, if you successfully advance past this phase, you gain more maturity and strengthen your sense of self.

An identity crisis isn't always obvious to the person experiencing it. Yes, you may notice that something is different and uncomfortable. But unless you know what it entails, you might not understand what is happening.

So, how do you figure out if you have an identity crisis? Next are five critical signs of identity crisis in adolescence.

1. Questions relating to your basic understanding of who you are

Asking questions about aspects of yourself that make up who you are is one of the critical signs of an identity crisis. For instance, you might question basic things about your character. *Am I a kind person? Am I an honest person? Would people describe me as a person of integrity? Am I an intelligent person?*

You might also ask questions about specific traits that define how you see yourself. For example, you might question whether you are an introvert, whether people find you agreeable, and whether you're easy to get along with.

Finally, you might ask questions about what matters most to you. You may wonder if you're truly passionate about certain things you believe to be your driving force. You may question your life purpose and whether it differs from what you believed it was.

2. Anxiety and dissatisfaction with life

Identity crises are usually uncomfortable and distressing. Naturally, you may feel anxious about your thoughts and the changes you're going through as a teenager. Struggles with your identity can cause internal turmoil, making you anxious, agitated, and dissatisfied with your life's direction.

3. Changing yourself to suit your environment, relationships, or situation

During this phase of your life, it's normal for your values to change abruptly and frequently. Instead of maintaining the same identity in all situations, you change values and tendencies depending on who you are with, where you are, or the situation you find yourself in.

For example, if you're among studious and quiet peers, you become studious and quiet. And when you're among chatty and upbeat friends, you transform into a social type.

You let your environment and who you are with – rather than your personality and choices – determine who you are now. Additionally, you let your friendships and relationships define you.

You might change your appearance and hobbies to match those of your friends. You convince yourself that you like the same things as they do. Suppose your friends don't like certain things you like. In that case, you give these things up to fit in with them.

This tendency to change who you are according to your environment, situation, or relationship can cause radical changes in your beliefs and opinions. This may include major things such as religious beliefs and political opinions or merely your opinions on pop culture, fashion, and food.

You might even change your mind daily and never know what to expect from yourself from one day to the next. Whether you realize it or not, you are changing your opinions to please others and find a place to belong.

4. Difficulty answering questions about who you are

Suppose you meet someone new and begin a conversation with them. How would you feel if they asked you questions about yourself? Do you enjoy it? Or do you find it hard to come up with answers?

If being asked questions about yourself makes you uncomfortable, that could signify an identity crisis. To deal with this, you may have developed effective tactics for changing the subject or conversing about the other person and agreeing with everything they say.

5. Not trusting yourself to make good decisions

Because your sense of self, values, and beliefs are ever-changing during an identity crisis, you may feel that you can't make good decisions for yourself. As such, you may hesitate between options, never fully choosing.

And when you *do* make a decision, you second-guess yourself. As a result, you may change your mind multiple times. This can make you feel like a failure, causing your self-esteem to lower significantly.

An identity crisis is a critical phase of major change. Sadly, it's pretty easy to respond to this phase by making changes that can negatively impact your mental health and well-being. However, dealing with your identity crisis becomes easier once you identify these signs.

The best way to deal with an identity crisis is to figure out your identity. And this is possible only if you embark on a self-discovery journey.

Next, let's look at some reasons for you to embark on a self-discovery journey.

Why Embark on a Self-Discovery Journey as a Teen?

"What if I had the opportunity to start discovering who I truly was from my teenage years?" "What if I took the time to look past my fears and find my true nature?" "If I learned self-acceptance and autonomy as a teen, how much different would my 20s and 30s be?"

These are some of the questions I get from adults currently going through a midlife identity crisis. And my answer is typically a variation of, "I'm sure things would be very different now."

Not everyone is courageous enough in adolescence to start scratching the surface and getting to know who they are. Indeed, many *adults* consider self-exploration an intense, daunting, and unnecessary task.

These people don't realize that the benefits of knowing oneself far outweigh their reasons for avoiding it. Self-discovery changes our lives and prepares us for success.

Learning as much as possible about your gifts, strengths, weaknesses, interests, inclinations, beliefs, and values may seem unimportant. But the key to living a rich and fulfilling life lies in exploring these things and forming a strong sense of self.

Self-discovery allows you to know yourself. When this happens, you get to unleash and own your inner power. You learn to seek and take advantage of opportunities that can help you reach your true potential.

Moreover, self-discovery allows you to recognize specific areas of your life that demand changes. At its core, self-exploration lays the foundation for personal development and satisfaction with life. It is the key to living a happy, healthy, and fulfilling life.

The journey toward self-discovery is non-linear, giving you an incredible opportunity to master patience and compassion. When you master these values, they change your approach to life and positively influence your relationship with others.

Remember that everyone is continually going through self-discovery and learning about themselves with every new experience. This should encourage you to extend empathy and compassion toward yourself as you navigate the process.

Do not think of self-discovery as a goal you must achieve by a deadline. Instead, accept it as a lifelong journey of exploring and uncovering layers of yourself and using the insights you obtain to transform into the best version of yourself.

Self-discovery will help:

- Support your psychological development
- Foster a strong sense of self
- Create a strong psychological foundation to help you face challenges and adversities
- Support your taking charge of your own life
- Encourage self-reliance and self-sufficiency

- Foster independent thinking and intelligence
- Support your discovery of career and life paths

It's important to embark on a self-exploration and self-discovery journey to become your desired adult. So, let's discuss some tips to help you kick off your journey the right way.

Tips to Help Kick Off Your Self-Discovery Journey

If you've reached that point where you wonder who you are, self-discovery is the key to getting to know yourself better. I know it sounds like a huge, overwhelming concept, but the process is as simple as:

- Examining your life
- Recognizing what's missing
- Taking steps toward self-fulfillment

There's no better time for self-discovery than your teenage years, so here are six tips to help you start the process.

1. Visualize your ideal self

So far, your life might be going pretty smoothly according to guidelines from parents, teachers, peers, and others. If this is the case, you probably haven't thought much about your true self. Sadly, many people define themselves by their relationships and the things they've accomplished without ever considering anything else.

If you don't understand what matters to you and the adult you hope to become, you will live for others rather than yourself.

You don't need to form a complete picture of who you want to become right now—after all, self-exploration is a lifelong journey. Still, try to answer the following questions:

- What do I want from life?
- Where do I want to be in five or ten years from now?
- What do I like about myself?

Answering these questions can be an excellent place to begin self-exploration.

2. Explore your passions

Passion gives life purpose and meaning. Some doctors are guided to medicine by a passion for helping people. Your passions don't have to be complex or career driven. Think about the things you enjoy spending time on. What excites you and makes you happy?

Exploring your interest in movies, books, and music can be a great way to get insight into your passions. Consider the things you enjoy most and look forward to. This can help you figure out how best to enrich your life.

3. Be curious

My favorite thing about self-exploration is that it can happen anywhere, at any time. All you need is to be genuinely and actively interested in yourself. As you go through life, take random moments to ask yourself uncomfortable questions. Explore happiness, purpose, grief, and similar concepts in your way.

Ask questions and meditate on them until you come up with satisfactory answers. Do not judge or discredit your experiences. Subsequently, you will see how these insights can help you uncover layers of yourself. Seemingly irrelevant or trivial experiences and memories can shed light on your beliefs, values, and feelings.

Some questions you can ask yourself include the following:

- What drives me?
- What am I missing out on?
- How do my choices impact the life I want for myself?
- Why do I engage in the activities I engage in?

Now, apply these questions to areas of your life. Note that you don't have to come up with answers immediately. Self-exploration takes time, and it helps to carefully consider your responses instead of writing down the first thing that comes to mind.

Be honest with yourself. The inability to come up with good answers does not indicate failure. It simply means you need to change the questions you're asking.

4. Write down your experiences

It helps to record your experiences as you go through life. You can do this by keeping a journal or getting a camera to help you retain memories. Journaling opens up a path to emotional release.

Recording your experiences via journaling allows you to articulate and understand your feelings and experiences objectively and without judgment. It offers you a chance to acknowledge how you feel, de-stress, and devise a way to address your concerns or problems effectively.

Additionally, it allows you to identify behavioral patterns and uncover layers of your subconscious. So, use 15 or 20 minutes daily to write down your feelings in a personal journal. Suppose you don't know what to write. In that case, keep a log of your everyday interactions and experiences. Doing this will allow you to reflect, structure your experiences, and gain new perspectives.

5. Try new things

At this stage of your life, it's OK if you can't name many passions. But you can start figuring this out by trying new things. Trying new adventures is the best way to figure out what you enjoy.

Perhaps you sense an interest in artistic pursuits. If so, join local communities that offer learning classes for teens. If you can't find a local community, take your search online. Joining an online class can give you enough insight to know if you want to keep pursuing this hobby or passion.

Exploring new things can feel overwhelming, depending on how adventurous they are. If you feel anxious, consider how proud you'll feel after accomplishing this new milestone. It can also be a great boost to your self-esteem.

6. Identify your values

Your values are certain qualities you consider most important and meaningful. They can reveal a lot about who you truly are. Personal values can paint a picture of the life you want for yourself and the behavior you expect from people.

Values typically include compassion, loyalty, honesty, courage, creativity, intelligence, etc. Clarifying what your values are can help you ensure you live them out. Exploring the most valuable things in life can make your self-discovery process much easier and more successful.

Self-discovery often leads to profound revelations about oneself. As you begin the journey, you will encounter discouraging phases. One of these phases is the rise of silent negative voices in your head.

The next chapter explores negative voices and how best to challenge them as you navigate self-exploration.

Step Two
Silent Negative Voices

Did you know that it's so easy for your ears to pick up words and sentences and your brain to be too sharp to digest them?

What you say to yourself is a big part of how you feel about yourself. When you have thoughts such as, *I am such a failure* or *I will never make genuine friendships*, these are negative voices that can hurt your self-esteem.

When your brain begins to see loopholes where they aren't, it's working on overdrive, and that's when you get fed with negative voices. These voices tell you stories you want to hear, holding you back from reaching your full potential.

When you fear how the world works, your beliefs will shape how you act and the interpretation of things happening to you. These beliefs can limit, hold you back, and sabotage your life dreams.

This chapter will discuss what negative voices and thoughts are and how to overcome them.

What Are Negative Voices/Limiting Beliefs?

Negative voices, also called negative thoughts or limiting beliefs, are thinking patterns in which you expect the worst possible outcome from people, situations, and events. Psychologists call them cognitive distortions, and they are very common in teenagers. They are perceptions, desires, and assumptions about oneself, others, and the world that are linked with unpleasant emotions and negative behavioral and physiological well-being.

Negative voices are usually triggered by fear of the future, anxiety about the present, and shame about the past. Before delving into that, know that negative voices aren't real. Those voices in your head that see the worst in every situation aren't real. Everyone gets one of those sometimes. However, it would be best not to let them become too loud in your head. Be in charge.

Now, to solve a problem, you've got to know the root of it so that you can uproot it. Let's look at the triggers of negative voices—fear of the future, anxiety about the present, and shame about the past.

Fear of the future:
You're young and bubbly, with many hormonal changes going on, and you're becoming more aware of the outside world through your friends, school, and family. That's already a lot for any teenager to handle. Everything around you looks so jam-packed that you feel the air leaving you, which is when negative thoughts set in.

Here are examples of how fear of the future can set in.

- You're moving and need to change schools and friends and then adjust to a new environment and lifestyle. It's normal to feel out of place, alone, and sad. But it's abnormal to feel like you're the problem or the people in the new community are the problem.

- You're rounding up high school, and your grades don't look too promising. Studying has always been a problem, so you're worried about what college you'll get into. You're worried you may not even get into college. You're worried, and it's fine. What's not cool is thinking that you're a failure because all your friends have already entered college, and you're not going to.

- Your parents have just announced that they'll be getting divorced. You're sad and heartbroken, and that's totally normal. But it becomes wrong when you start to see yourself as the reason for the divorce.

- You keep changing schools because you get bullied. You feel alone and scared, but you aren't alone. You're right to be skeptical of anyone who tries to get close to you, but that doesn't mean you should shut yourself off from the world. It gets messed up when you blame yourself for other people's terrible behavior toward you.

- You're young and innocent, yet you've received a life-changing diagnosis. It's normal to get depressed, sad, and lonely. You don't deserve any such illness at a tender age, and it's not your fault. It worsens when you accept the illness as fate and blame yourself or others for it.

Anxiety about the present:
There's a lot of pressure on teenagers in today's world. If it's not on the internet, it's in the classroom and even at home. It's normal to get overwhelmed by external pressure, but that's

about how much we should take. Adding internal pressure to it can lead to intrusive, negative thoughts.

- You experience changes in your mood and body. The emotional changes during puberty for girls have not really been explored as well as the physical changes. The changes you experience are totally normal. Comparing your growth to others is inevitable, but you shouldn't get engulfed by it. When you begin berating yourself because you're not meeting a standard set by the media, that becomes a problem.

- Another reason to overthink in the present and conceive negative thoughts is bullying. Bullying affects the future and the present and eventually becomes a shameful past. It is important to remember that you're not to blame for other people's cruddy behavior. When you begin to say mean things to yourself, that's a problem.

- Excessive worry about the present can be stressful. You feel lost for words as to how you really feel. It can be confusing and difficult to navigate, leading to anger because your heart feels tight most of the time. Then you become quiet, angry, and sad, and sometimes you hear negative voices criticizing you or others because of those emotions.

Shame about the past:
You can feel insecure about a past event, even at a tender age. However, the past must be left alone, exactly where it belongs. It's normal to feel sad about the past, but your past – no matter how ugly it may be – is never something to be constantly ashamed of. Accept your past, and just let it be.

- Perhaps, your shame is about a parent, and the gossip never ends. Whatever mistake your parents made, you don't need to feel bad about that. It's something out of your control and nothing you should feel ashamed of or blame the world for.

- When it's about an illness, it's not something to think deeply about. An illness is nobody's fault; therefore, you don't need to feel ashamed.

How Limiting Beliefs Can Affect You as a Teen

Negative emotions and intrusive negative thoughts are normal and experienced by everyone. Still, for you, the constant presence of these thoughts can cause symptoms of major mental illnesses that demand medical attention.

It's okay to get angry, sad, lonely, and feel cheated. These emotions spring up after a negative event, but you shouldn't let them fester. Push them aside, and do not dwell on them so much to the extent it begins to affect your day-to-day activities.

Dwelling on negative thoughts can lead to and show symptoms of:

Oppositional Defiant Disorder – You're easily angered when things don't go your way. You're opposed to a higher authority and feel like rules are there to challenge or hold you down. You don't know why you feel this way and react that way, and no one second-guesses you.

Depression and Anxiety – Carrying around a bagful of negative emotions and thoughts eventually leads down this road. You become a hermit, angry with the world. It causes you to lose friends and family and, eventually, takes too much from you at an early age. It can be painful to process, but it's not the end of the world.

Obsessive Compulsive Disorder – Negative emotions and thoughts fuel mental illnesses. As mentioned earlier, negative thoughts are cognitive distortions, and when they are repetitive, that becomes a problem. This can affect your day-to-day activities and how you talk to people.

Limiting beliefs can stunt your chances of enjoying your teenage years. The first thing to realize is that those thoughts aren't real, so there's no need to give them a chance to rule. Your teenage years are precious, so don't spend them wallowing in depression, anxiety, or mental illness. You've got a lot of years ahead of you, and you're still going to meet bigger challenges ahead. So, build a strong mind to safeguard yourself from negative thoughts. Not that you won't get them, but at least they'll have no chance of controlling your life or influencing your decisions.

You may wonder what kinds of thoughts are okay and what kinds are not, since sometimes, negative thoughts may sound realistic and logical to you.

Here is a list of how your thoughts can be negative.

- *Thinking you've messed everything up and it's all your fault*
- *Telling yourself you'll be single until you die because a prospect turned you down*
- *Thinking you're ugly because a certain crush ignored or rejected you for not being their type*
- *Telling yourself you belong in the gutter after something you've been working hard for doesn't work out*
- *Turning down and running away from projects because you're convinced you'll bring bad luck to the team just because a similar effort you've tried in the past didn't work out*
- *Tending to always blame others*
- *Seeing a problem in every suggested solution*

- *Seeing yourself as a failure after you fail to meet a personal target*
- *Hating yourself for falling back into an old habit*
- *Expecting the worst in everyone and never accepting a compliment*

These thoughts may seem healthy initially because you think you're trying to protect yourself from getting hurt. You think by being hard on yourself, you're somehow very upright. But blaming yourself unnecessarily is as unfair as blaming others when they're innocent. Treat yourself better. You're all you've got in the end, so who will be there for *you* if you aren't?

I know adolescence can be scary and overwhelming, but who says you can't flip it around and enjoy your teenage years? There are so many fun things for you to do. There are friends to make, places to visit, books to read, content to create, etc. All these can't be thrown down in front of negative thoughts.

Thinking positively may seem challenging because you believe optimistic people are either naive or intentionally ignorant. Optimists see the good in every situation rather than the bad. It's easier to focus on the bad, but focusing on the good requires extra courage, and that's what optimists project. They have a sense of courage that everything will turn out fine, but even if it doesn't, they'll keep being awesome. They don't let a bad day evolve into a bad life. They are at peace with their emotions and are more than aware that the negative thoughts aren't real. This makes it easier for them to flip those thoughts around and take back the reins whenever they set in.

Strategies to Overcome Negative Voices/Limiting Beliefs

You may wonder, how do I flip these thoughts around? What strategies do I need to put these thoughts in their place and live my life to the fullest as a teenage girl? The answers to that question are as follows:

Know those voices are not real

The naysayers are not real; they're made up and fake. You can't see them because they're not even real. That's the first step to getting rid of them. See them as something you can dispose of; something unreal and unneeded. It's very possible, even though it's not easy. But once you can say *"It's not real"* to yourself and mean it, you'll be ready for the next step.

Pick up a habit

To get rid of a habit, you've got to replace it with something else. Exercising is a perfect way to help your mind cleanse and drown out these voices. Whoever said teenage girls don't need exercise? It doesn't have to be anything hard. It can be a simple run, light pushups, rope skipping, lifting dumbbells, or just stretching. It could even be yoga. The tranquility and fluidity aspect of yoga is the perfect healing requirement to kill those voices.

Write them down and replace them with better things

When you blame yourself for something out of your control, encourage yourself for a job well done and decide to do better next time. Replace "It's my fault" with "I didn't give it my best this time. I'll do way better next time." Replacing negative energy with positive energy doesn't mean you excuse yourself of faults when it's clearly on you. It just means that you're more rational and understanding. It means you're willing to give yourself another chance.

Know that it's not you and not them—it just happened
Understand that some things just happen. The separation of your parents is not your fault. It's not your fault that the adults want to go their separate ways, or you learned about a growth disorder at an early age. It can happen to anyone. You're not unlucky, and you deserve better. It's not your fault or your family's either. Instead of apportioning blame in situations like this, focusing on the solution is better when the situation is something like an illness. For divorce cases, moving on and adapting to the situation is a positive energy needed.

Talk to people close to you
You're new to this. You've got a lot happening in your head. It's not the time to keep quiet. It would help to let people around you know what's happening in your headspace. Your parents might feel weirded out when you start acting funny because of the voices. However, when you talk to them, they'll be more informed on how to help you in a crisis. Besides your family, it might help if you talked to a professional. They will give you authentic means to get rid of the voices. If you're not the type that likes to talk a lot, find that one person you're comfortable with and fill them in on what's going on. Either way, talk it out and let someone know.

Journal
Here, you get to write down some important things about your day. One of these things should be the way you're feeling. Writing down these feelings helps you evaluate them. I said

earlier to write down the negative thoughts and replace them with positive words. Here, you're not writing the negative thoughts but how you feel—suffocated, left behind, teary, grateful, sad, etc. You write all of those down and try to access your feelings and understand them.

Forgive yourself

Life isn't always black and white. Cut yourself some slack because you're still young. You don't need to be so hard on yourself. Comparison is the greatest thief of joy. There's no rationale behind comparison, whether it's body proportions, grades, or looks. Comparing only makes us set unreasonable deadlines for ourselves and end up not meeting them. You've got a whole life to live out there. Embrace your weaknesses and move on.

Practice compassionate self-talk

This may seem awkward, but besides the initial step, this is highly crucial for silencing hostile voices. Soothe yourself with compassionate self-talk when the voices come swelling into your head, yelling at you for not doing anything. Tell yourself what you'd tell someone else who's emotionally down. This isn't a self-pity stunt. Instead, it's real life and one solution to the negative thoughts that have worked over the decades.

The list can go on and on. You may even think of some later, but that's all right. Most importantly, you're consciously working to eliminate those negative thoughts. The negative voices in your head are not real and deserve no right to rule your world. You're the monarch of your life, and you should sit on that throne like a Queen.

Finally, a victory over negative voices is a victory over depression, anxiety, fear, and abandonment. It's a victory against the naysayers and a launch into your potential as a power teen girl.

Step Three
Manage Complex Emotions

Pause for a moment and think about what's happening in your mind right now. How do you feel at this moment?

Your emotions are what make you feel. They give you information about what you're going through and also help you know how you should react to it.

The subject of emotions is crucial because whatever is going on in your life at any given time generates emotions within you that determine how you respond to the situation. Suppose something drastic just happened. Having processed the information about the occurrence, you may react by feeling sad, happy, encouraged, angry, confused, bored, distracted, indifferent, or something else. That happens because of your emotions; they're alive and active within every human being.

Here we'll be focusing on how you can manage the inevitable complex emotions you'll experience as a teen.

What Are Emotions?

Emotions, as defined by Britannica, are bodily sensations, behavior, and complex feelings of consciousness reflecting the personal importance of an event or situation. Also, the American Psychological Association (APA) defines emotions as *"a complex reaction pattern involving experiential, behavioral, and physiological elements."*

Though you may not have been conscious of it, you have been aware of your emotions since you were a baby. As a child, you could feel and respond to your surroundings. Your emotions were responsible for your facial expressions; the times you smiled back at your mom, cried because you were hungry, and were confused about your new toy are all times you expressed your emotions. However, you couldn't put a name on them.

You became better at understanding your emotions as you grew up. As a teen, you no longer react to things as you did when you were a child. You can now correctly identify your feelings toward things and circumstances and translate those feelings into words. Over time, as you experience different feelings, you become emotionally aware of them and why you feel that way.

There is a need for emotional awareness as it helps you understand what you want. You can also know you *don't* like something when you have emotional awareness. So, you do better in your relationships because you can state your feelings clearly. That helps you overcome your relationship difficulties since you can resolve your conflicts more quickly and better.

Not everyone has emotional awareness. However, with some practice, everyone can develop it. Emotional awareness is adequately controlling your emotions, which helps you succeed in your life endeavors.

Emotions are generally classified as basic or complex.

Basic emotions are direct emotions. Your facial expressions quickly identify them. They are also spontaneous because you don't think them through before expressing them. If you were to see a viper while walking in the field, your first and sudden emotion would be fear, and it will be written all over you. Anyone looking at you can tell that you are afraid of something. That's what basic emotions are, and there are six of them: fear, anger, sadness, surprise, happiness, and disgust.

Complex emotions, on the other hand, are not easily identified. People cannot quickly tell them from the look on your face. Examples are regret, grief, jealousy, guilt, and envy. Others are worry, pride, gratitude, and embarrassment. Complex emotions can also be a combination of two or more emotions. For example, hate can spring up due to anger, disgust, and fear. Hate is not also easily recognized on the face. That's because complex emotions may not even have any facial expression accompanying them in some individuals. Again, the way people express complex emotions differs in various places. For example, different people and cultures have different ways of showing grief. While some cry a lot of the time, others may sit on the ground without saying much for hours and even days.

Some other complex emotions may not have any facial expressions with which you can quickly identify them. An excellent example of that is jealousy. These are silent emotions you feel within you. Still, because of the circumstances involved, you may be careful not to tell anyone exactly how you feel.

Teenagers struggle with many complex emotions because they're at a stage where most things seem rather complicated. The world doesn't seem so simple and innocent anymore as it did when you viewed it years back with your childlike eyes.

As you experience different changes in your body and mind, you also experience other emotions you cannot easily express most of the time.

Have you ever been happy and sad at the same time about something? Let's say a dear friend is going to college overseas. You're delighted that she finally got admitted into her chosen school to study her preferred course. Both of you dream of achieving success in the future and working in your preferred fields of endeavor. Your friend has just reached one of the significant steps to making her dreams a reality. Of course, this makes you happy. But then, having to see her go far away to a foreign country to study makes you sad because she's been part of your life, and you hate that you will no longer get to see her anytime you want to.

How about those times when you like someone and don't like them at the same time? When someone asks you what's going on, you explain it as "It's complicated!" Sound familiar? These are all complex emotions, and the teenage years are when you begin to understand them.

When you were much younger, your feelings were mainly basic, and life seemed easier. You also made choices more quickly. However, adolescence makes you question almost everything and makes you aware of other ways to respond to situations. That puts you against the world often as you suddenly see things differently from the way others see them. You want what others feel you shouldn't have and want to do things differently.

Here are two vital points you should know about your emotions.

Emotions are not permanent. They do not stay after you experience them. Emotions are temporal. They may last for an extended period or a short while. On a typical day, you will encounter several emotions—all of them different from each other. Various occurrences will make you feel happy, angry, sad, and excited all in one day. So, you must know that emotions will come and go. Parting ways with a close friend will leave you heartbroken for a while, depending on how deep the relationship was. But you will soon forget about the heartbreak once you become close to someone else. The heartbreak lasts for a while but is eventually replaced with love.

Emotions have different intensities. You feel one emotion deeply, while you may feel others just mildly. It all depends on the circumstances involved. For example, if you hear on the news that a car crash occurred somewhere in your city, you will naturally feel sad about what happened. However, this sadness may not be so intense because you haven't heard that anyone you know is among those hurt in the crash. The feeling will be more intense if you discover one of your friends or neighbors is in that crash. You will suddenly experience a flush of emotions—sadness, panic, and anxiety. You want to know if your friend or neighbor survived the crash. Your hands shake as you reach for the phone to make calls. Your heartbeat starts to race as you think about the best person to call. You are experiencing loads of emotions, and they're so intense.

The Role of Emotions on Your Mindset

Mindset is your perception or belief about yourself or any other thing. It is the way you view things. The mindset you develop is how "YOU" have trained your mind to perceive those things. You form a mindset about anything mainly because of how you "feel" or "think" about it at certain times. That's emotion.

There is a significant connection between your emotions and mindset. How you "feel and think" will determine how you "perceive." While you may be right in how your feelings make you perceive things, you may be wrong at other times. Again, while the fusion of your emotions and mindset can help you attain your goals, they may be the architect of your not reaching your heights.

It's easy for people to develop a certain mindset just because of how they've felt in prior circumstances. That's what makes them have preferences. For example, you prefer going to a specific coffee shop because you think their customer service is superb. The attendants are so polite and always smiling. You like how they make you feel whenever you go there and automatically acclaim them as the best. You can easily refer that shop to your friends because you've developed a mindset about it.

When you *don't* like something, it's probably because of how it makes you feel. If your mindset about something is good or bad, it's because of how you feel about it. The only way to overcome your limitations is to have the right mindset. Yes, your mindset can limit you from attaining your full potential, and maybe you need to change your perspective about some things. However, to change your perspective about anything, you must first change how you feel or think about them. Your emotions must change. Only then can you change your mindset and break the limitations.

Your emotions and mindset control your level of confidence and self-esteem. If you think you're not smart, you will form that perception of yourself with time. It will make you look down on yourself when you are with your friends. You'll feel lesser than others because you've developed that mindset of not being good enough. However, once you change your thoughts and focus more on your positive attributes, you will begin to perceive yourself more positively. Then your confidence will start to rise.

You must be mindful of your emotions to attain your full potential as a teenage girl. You must be careful of how you see yourself. You must be happy with yourself first before anyone else. When you treat yourself right, you will have the right mindset about yourself. The right attitude is what energizes you to fulfill your dreams and aspirations.

While writing this, I was a little distracted at some point by a lady sharing her experience on TV about life with an autistic child. According to her, they discovered early that their first child was autistic, and raising her has been challenging (she's now 18). In those early stages of dealing with an autistic child, she became terrified of getting pregnant again because she feared having these issues again. Years later, she almost passed out when the doctor told her she was pregnant! Luckily, she's had two other children in addition to the first, and they're both okay—all teenagers now. What a relief!

Looking at that lady's experience in the light of what we're discussing, she developed a mindset of not wanting any more children because of the experiences that instilled fear in her. The "fear" emotion influenced her so much that she formed a mindset of not wanting more children. Her sentiment was going to shape the rest of her life forever. It almost made her lose the chance of having the happy and beautiful family she has today. She explained that the birth of her two other daughters brought so much hope and strength to handle the needs of her first child. Also, her mindset of other kids being autistic was proved wrong with the coming of her other kids. As mentioned earlier, this shows that some perspectives can deprive us of attaining our full potential. Unfortunately, those mindsets stay with us over time due to our harboring of negative emotions.

You must maintain good self-esteem and confidence and have a positive mindset. Your perceptions must be correct for you to achieve your goals. More importantly, it would help if you got your emotions right. You have your whole life ahead of you and deserve to make something good out of it. A positive mindset and upbeat emotions are vital as you go through this phase.

What Are the Growing Pains of Hormonal Changes?

It's very common for you to have changes in emotions. You could be happy this minute, and the next minute you're downcast. You could be having a hearty conversation one minute and want to be alone the next minute. You don't have to be confused about whether something is wrong with you. It's perfectly normal to face mood swings as a teen. However, on rare occasions, it may be an underlying symptom of a more severe problem.

Hormonal changes are reasons you may act in ways you don't understand as a teen. They are mainly responsible for all those mood swings. As you develop, you experience some emotions, such as sadness, recurrent frustration, and irritability, in extreme measures.

Hormones are chemical substances produced by the glands in your body. They are "chemical messengers," as most people refer to them. They are responsible for maintaining the body's homeostasis, meaning they help the body regulate itself properly. During the teenage years, your body produces a hormone known as gonadotropin. This hormone activates the production of other hormones—growth, adrenal, and sex. These hormones are produced in increased amounts during the teenage years, affecting the body differently.

Below are some aspects in which hormones cause significant changes:

Body: A spike in hormones during puberty makes you experience changes in your body. As a teenage girl, you start to develop breasts, your hips get fuller, hair starts to grow under your arms and in your private parts, and you also notice changes in your voice. You may sweat more than usual, and your underarms may not smell fresh. You will also start menstruating because your reproductive organ has been activated.

Mood: As part of the hormonal changes in your body, you will experience a lot of mood swings. You will easily change from one mood to the other. You may get temperamental occasionally, making others wonder what's wrong with you. You will also want to keep more to yourself in these years. You may get weary of the company you used to enjoy because something within you tells you, "You're way bigger than that now!"

Emotions: As a teenager, you will experience new emotions, most of which are complex. You gradually lose your "childish innocence" and begin to read between the lines more often. While you forgave quickly as a child, you will start to examine things more deeply as a teen and find letting go rather difficult. You become more aware of complex emotions like jealousy, hate, and love. You also begin to develop a different kind of liking for the opposite sex. You don't see them the way you used to see them—as children. You tend to like them differently, and you may even get butterflies when one you like smiles at you! It's okay; there's nothing wrong with you. It's just one of the many things you go through due to hormonal changes. Every adult experienced the same things when they were teens.

Impulses: You may start acting on impulse now. You want to do something and feel strongly about it, even when others think otherwise. As a teen, I woke up one day and decided I wanted a pet rabbit. Before my parents could tell me their feelings, I was already crying for one! Till today, I don't know why I wanted rabbits! So, don't feel bad when you begin to act like that; you may be reacting to hormone changes.

Hormonal Imbalance

While it's normal to see these changes in your body and mind during adolescence due to hormonal changes, there are cases where some teens experience hormonal imbalances. This can lead to serious health challenges.

Hormonal imbalance is a result of your body producing abnormal levels of hormones. There may be too few or too many hormones in your bloodstream. When not produced at normal levels, the effect on the body can be significant. Some major causes of hormonal imbalance are:

- Genetics
- Prolonged stress
- Steroid abuse
- Poor nutrition
- Unhealthy lifestyle
- Inadequate sleep
- Environmental factors

Hormonal Imbalance Can Have the Following Effects

1. Exposure to mental health issues

With other factors leading to stress, hormonal imbalance can expose teenagers to mental health issues. It can lead to disorder in the way the brain functions. That happens because the stress hormone receptors are increased while relaxation hormones are reduced. As a result, you experience ongoing anxiety.

2. Adrenal hormone problems

It's common for teenagers to experience mood swings and stress occasionally. However, it's abnormal for the stress hormone called cortisol to increase in production. That can affect how the body deals with stress, leading to adrenaline anxiety problems.

3. Mood and behavioral problems

As mentioned earlier, sex hormones increase during the teenage years. In both boys and girls, testosterone and estrogen are the leading sex hormones produced in the body. When there is an imbalance in the production of these hormones, the body suffers side effects such as depression, irritability, anxiety, low self-esteem, lack of confidence, confusion, and social withdrawal.

What to Do When Your Emotions Are Out of Control

1. Slow down

Your emotions may be uncontrollable because you've been too consumed with activities. Being too busy and getting stressed can make you feel so overwhelmed that you lose touch with yourself. All you're concerned about is how to get things done. You may also begin to go overboard with your temperament because you're burning out so fast. It would help if you slowed down. Breathe and get the hang of yourself. Step back and evaluate things properly before continuing your usual activities.

2. Meditate

Meditation helps you find a balance, which is just what you need to calm your emotions. It removes the noisiness from your head and makes you more focused and assertive. Enroll with a teacher or watch meditation videos online. Meditate whenever you are overwhelmed and don't know how to handle things.

3. Listen to music

Music is calming, especially when you feel confused or stressed. Listen to your favorite playlist when your emotions are running wild.

4. Turn to a creative hobby

Creativity helps you feel calm and in better control of your emotions. It's also an opportunity to eliminate negative emotions and feel lighter. When your emotions are out of control, paint a picture, draw something, or engage in any creative exercises you prefer.

5. Count

I've always loved counting from one to thirty when I felt I was losing it. Counting helps you slow down your actions when you're already out of control with your emotions. Chances are you'll say or do something not so objective in such a state. Counting will help delay your subsequent actions borne out of insufficient thought processes. By the time you finish counting, you will have gotten a hold of yourself and will likely think better.

6. Go to a quiet place

If you're having emotional trouble, it may help to escape the noise and go to a solitary place where you can enjoy quiet. This will allow you to think things through and take better action.

7. Do not suppress your emotions further

While it's bad enough that you're not so much in control of your emotions at this time, it would help if you let out the hurt inside somehow. Some people cry while others loudly scream with a pillow over their mouths. Do any of these or find something safe and healthy that works for you. The idea is to quickly empty your mind of the negative emotions choking you.

Strategies for Emotional Regulation for Teens

You can adopt the following strategies to regulate your emotions:

1. Eat a healthy diet

Eat healthily to maintain a good emotional state. Eating meals high in carbohydrates and fat can make you feel drained and less active. You should eat more fruits and vegetables and reduce junk foods from your diet as much as possible. Whole grains are also healthy for you.

2. Sleep adequately

Teenagers are known to stay up late at night. They love to watch late-night movies rather than get a sound sleep. When you deprive yourself of adequate sleep, you can develop emotional problems. This can make you get upset quickly and become irritable. Doctors recommend that you sleep at least eight hours every night.

3. Find time to rest

As a teen, you will burst with so much energy that you can become involved in many activities simultaneously. Many teens work part-time while schooling, get involved in sporting activities, volunteer on weekends, and still find time to hang out with friends. Being too busy can make you overwhelmed and irritable. It will help if you find time to rest in between these activities. While it's good to be social and get involved, it'll also do you some good to have some alone time when you relax your mind and get refreshed.

4. Keep a journal of your emotions

Keep a journal in which you write down your emotions daily. Write about your happy moments as well as your worries and disappointments. Emptying yourself into the journal every day will help you feel better. You can also keep a gratitude journal, in which you write down something you're grateful for each day.

5. Exercise daily

Everyone knows how important exercise is to the body. Exercising can prevent illnesses like diabetes, cancer, and other severe health conditions. Exercising will also help you maintain good mental health. Exercise is an excellent way to deal with complex emotions like anxiety, depression, and irritability. It enables you to keep your mind clear so you can think properly.

6. Talk to someone you trust

It is very common for teens to hide things from their parents. They want to conceal what they're going through most of the time. If you ever feel that you are getting out of control with your emotions or having problems with school, work, or any other area of your life, you should talk to someone you trust.

Please speak to your mom or dad. Open up to someone you respect and admire. You will get valuable advice to guide you in any problematic situation.

Step Four
Develop Resilience

Everyone needs tools to navigate hard times and distressing emotions. Teenagers need resilience because adolescence is a period of intense change and difficulty. Every teen has a different temperament, so it's important to find a way to build resilience and become more purposeful and positive.

Resilience means adapting to stress, challenge, trauma, adversity, or emotional suffering. As a teenager, there will be points in your life where you'll face issues, difficulties, and challenges. This is a normal part of life.

Your parents or friends often say, "Be strong; you'll pull through," or "You should be more resilient." What does this mean? And how do you achieve this in a practical sense?

What Is Resilience?

According to the US Department of Health and Human Services, resilience is *"the ability to withstand, adapt to, and recover from adversity and stress."* Being resilient means being able to overcome and bounce back from a difficult experience or situation. It is picking yourself up after a traumatic or painful experience.

Your resilience level will change and grow throughout your life. It's OK if, at some point, you notice that you don't cope with difficult situations as well as others. And sometimes, you might surprise yourself when you navigate a difficult situation well. You can also think of resilience as a psychological tool to help you return to feeling normal after a major change.

Even as a teen, you may have noticed that when you're in a weakened position in which it feels as if things are getting progressively worse, it can be hard to find your balance or regain stability. Resilience is how you achieve this.

Being resilient doesn't mean you don't experience sadness, disappointment, failure, or other negative emotions. However, it means you *will* bounce back from these experiences more easily.

Two teenagers can experience the same situation, and one emerges unaffected while the other falls down a depressive hole. Much of how you react to situations is determined by teen resilience—how quickly and easily you rebound from stress or challenge and return to your normal level of well-being.

Many biological, environmental, and psychological factors affect how teens react to distressing events and circumstances. However, there are tools to help you cultivate resilience and develop greater inner strength.

Resilience is closely linked to mental health. Building your ability to adapt in the face of challenges or adversity can help you heal more quickly from anxiety, depression, trauma, and other mental health conditions and difficult experiences.

I read a study conducted with junior high and high school students in China in 2020. It found that adolescents with greater resilience had better mental health during the 2020 pandemic than their peers.

Resilience infuses you with positive emotions, self-compassion, and overall well-being. It makes you less likely to turn to destructive coping mechanisms such as substance abuse, eating disorders, self-harm, and other unhealthy habits.

A lack of resilience can make you fixate on problems, become overwhelmed, or victimize yourself. I'm not saying resilience will make your problems disappear—it won't. But it can make you see beyond your problems, find happiness in the little things, manage stress effectively, and pursue enjoyment in life.

What are some benefits of resilience?

- Improved academic achievement
- Reduced absences from studies due to illness
- Reduced risk of unhealthy habits and destructive behaviors
- Increased commitment to family or community activities
- Lower mortality rate and increased physical health

Life experiences – including illness, natural disasters, family or relationship problems, bullying, major accidents, traumatic events, abuse, or losing a loved one – can challenge or test your resilience.

You will naturally struggle with painful emotions when you go through a crisis. No matter what, you must allow yourself to fully experience those feelings, knowing that they will eventually pass. Reminding yourself that happier times will come is the key to coping with stressful life events and building resilience. Again, resilience is a vital life skill you can develop throughout your lifetime.

The question is, what does resilience look like?

What Does Being Resilient Look Like?

My transition from high school to college was the first major transition I experienced, and I practically fell on my face. Things had always come pretty easy for me, but college was a different ball game. I struggled in a way I wasn't familiar with. The degree I had chosen appeared to be out of my wheelhouse.

I studied hard, but it barely had any effect. I struggled with most aspects of my academics, especially the critiques and competition, because I was in a competitive field. In hindsight, what I went through wasn't particularly unique to me.

Many people face these challenges, but I didn't handle them as well as I should have. I may have earned my degree, but it was a difficult period. I even cried at my graduation party, believing I would never accomplish anything with my degree.

After this period, I promised myself I'd become stronger and sturdier for my next life phase. At the time, I didn't know I was discussing developing resilience. I did not know what resilience looked like.

Earlier, when I defined resilience, I'm sure a few people you know popped into your mind. That family friend who went through a difficult breakup ended up making their life better for it. Or the one who was laid off from work and, a few months later, made a comeback happier than ever.

If you're anything like the average teenager, you are probably inspired by the grace with which those people handled awful life events. It is a quality that you should admire and desire.

So, what does being resilient look like in action? A few examples of ways to show resilience include:

- Doing your best to take a positive perspective in any situation you encounter

- Approaching challenges as opportunities to learn

- Regulating your emotions and expressing your feelings appropriately

- Focusing on the things within your control rather than dwelling on those you cannot change

- Identifying your cognitive distortions and recognizing they aren't truths or facts

- Transforming negative thoughts into more positive and realistic ones

For example, suppose you get stuck in traffic on your way to school. A non-resilient person might become stressed out, angry, or worried about being late. However, if you're resilient, you might choose to learn from the situation. In that case, you might remind yourself to leave earlier for school or soothe yourself with the fact that you're usually on time.

When people talk about resilience, they refer to "emotional resilience." Most people are familiar with this term because it concerns our ability to manage the emotional effects of stress, adversity, and trauma.

However, many people aren't familiar with other types of resilience. You must develop these different types of resilience because you will need them at varying times.

- **Inherent resilience.** This is the kind of resilience we're all born with. An inborn resilience protects and informs you as you explore and learn more about the world. It teaches you to play, learn, and take risks. This resilience is most prevalent when you're under seven years of age (provided your development happens smoothly and without disruption).

- **Adapted resilience.** This resilience manifests at different points in life, usually due to a difficult or life-changing experience. Adaptive resilience occurs on-the-spot as a way for you to manage stress and pain effectively.

- **Learned resilience.** This resilience builds over time as you go through different situations and experiences. Then, it activates when you're faced with challenging situations. In a way, you learn when to draw on your learned resilience and apply it in stressful periods. You learn, grow, and build your mechanisms for managing painful experiences through it. It teaches you to draw on the inner strength you may not know you have, at the times you need it the most.

Other examples of what being resilient looks like include:

- Relying on others
- Trusting in your abilities
- Being kind and compassionate toward yourself
- Changing the stories you tell about yourself
- Taking the next step, no matter how small

Being resilient also involves understanding that life is riddled with challenges. While you may not be able to avoid life's many problems, you can be open, flexible, and willing to adapt according to your situation and circumstance.

Ingredients for Resilience

Self-awareness, self-discipline, self-control, problem-solving, and social support are the main ingredients for building resilience. A resilient person is in tune with situations, emotional reactions, and the behavior of everyone around them.

Awareness is how you maintain control of any situation you find yourself in and develop new ways of tackling your problems. By default, you become stronger after coming out unscathed from such difficult situations.

People may vary significantly in the coping skills they apply when facing a crisis. Still, researchers have highlighted some key characteristics that everyone who wants to build resilience must possess.

Many of these skills or "ingredients" can be strengthened over time, improving your ability to manage life's adversities and setbacks.

Here are the six basic ingredients of resilience.

1. Problem-solving skills

You need strong problem-solving skills to develop resilience. Usually, when there's a crisis, resilient people can come up with a solution that will produce a safe and favorable outcome. Meanwhile, non-resilient people get tunnel vision in stressful or dangerous situations. They might miss important details or fail to seize opportunities to create an advantage for themselves.

By strengthening your problem-solving skills, you can calmly and rationally assess a situation or problem and devise an effective solution.

2. Social support and connections

It helps to have people who can be your backbone and provide much-needed support whenever you struggle. Simply talking about the problem or challenge you're facing with other people can help you gain a fresh perspective and seek new solutions. It can also be a way for you to express how you feel.

Individuals with high resilience levels typically have a community of family members, friends, peers, and online groups to maintain their social connections. So, it would be best if you can build up your support network.

3. Emotional regulation

Resilience is characterized by the ability to effectively regulate one's emotions and those of others. You must recognize when you have an emotional reaction or response and identify the trigger for that reaction. This can help you better handle your emotions and manage the situation at hand effectively.

4. Survivor mentality

When faced with a potential crisis, you must consider yourself a survivor. Do not victimize yourself at any point. Resilient people don't think of themselves as victims in any circumstance. Instead, they find ways to solve their problems and *change* their circumstances. Even if the situation is unavoidable, highly resilient individuals remain focused on getting a positive outcome.

5. Self-compassion

A key part of resilience is treating yourself with compassion. The most resilient people I know are as compassionate toward themselves as they are toward other people. They recognize when it's time to take a break and can embrace their emotions, which is key to building and strengthening resilience.

Not only does self-compassion help to develop resilience, but it also boosts your overall health and well-being and prepares you for life's challenges and setbacks.

6. Sense of control

Do you feel like you have some degree of control over your life? Or do you constantly find external sources to blame for your problems and failures?

Resilient individuals generally possess what psychologists call an "internal locus of control." They believe that their actions determine the outcome of the situations they find themselves in.

Yes, some factors, such as natural disasters or accidents, are out of our control. While you may be able to blame external causes for your circumstance, it is still important to feel that the power to make decisions that can affect your situation, your ability to cope, and your future is within your control.

This is a key ingredient in developing and strengthening your resilience.

Improve Resilience with Positive Thinking

Do you ever notice that everything seems to go right when you begin the day in a good mood? You get to school early, have great conversations with your friends and peers, and answer questions brilliantly in class. Overall, your productivity is high, and you feel so good.

Such is the power of positive thinking. When you view situations from a positive perspective, you notice the good rather than the bad, boosting your ability to cope with stress and show resilience.

While some people are certainly more inclined to positive thinking than others, improving resilience with our thoughts is something we can all learn to do. You can improve your resilience by using the strategies I will share to cultivate positive thinking patterns.

Looking at what happens in brain chemistry, it's easy to understand how positive thoughts hold power over how we experience life and, in turn, our resilience levels. When confronted with criticism, rejection, or negativity – due to either your thought processes or the actions of others – your brain releases high levels of cortisol, the primary stress hormone.

Cortisol then shuts down your brain's thinking center and activates aggression, conflict aversion, and other suboptimal behaviors. In essence, it makes you more sensitive and reactive, and less rational. This impairs your ability to assess situations logically and objectively. As a result, you're primed to look for the negatives in a situation and magnify them.

In contrast, positive thoughts and interactions trigger the release of oxytocin, which activates neural pathways in the prefrontal cortex, the part of your brain responsible for improving communication and building trust.

Unfortunately, oxytocin doesn't stay in your bloodstream as long as cortisol; therefore, its positively wonderful effects don't last as long as the harmful effects of cortisol. To develop resilience, you must make consistent efforts to be positive.

While positive thinking can help you feel good now, it also rewires the brain long-term. Positive thinking can reframe the brain to be more positive and activate parts of the brain that can help to cultivate resilience.

In short, you can build and strengthen your resilience by cultivating a positive mindset. Start with small changes, be consistent over time, and you will notice a significant improvement in how you perceive and cope with challenges.

So, how do you cultivate a positive mindset?

- **Reframe your thoughts and perspectives.** Fortunately, you can choose how you embrace each day and situation. Adjust your frame by looking for opportunities, seeking solutions to your problem, and using positive language when assessing a situation. For example, don't say, "I can't handle this." Instead, say, "This is a difficult situation, but I can pull through. I have coped with worse difficulties in the past."

- **Look for the positives and practice gratitude.** Research suggests that taking a few minutes to focus on the positives in our life and express gratitude rewires the brain to develop a habit of seeking the positives rather than the negatives in any situation. So, take a moment to appreciate your parents and friends, the beautiful weather, your favorite movie, the food on your table, or that person who made you laugh today. If you are in a negative thinking pattern, pause and find the positives in the situation or your life. Express gratitude for three things in your life daily; this will rewire your brain to be more positive.

- **Change how you respond to stress.** It's not so much stress that affects us but how we view and react to it. Stress is a fact of life; it is inevitable. You're better off taking stress as an opportunity to make changes or grow in your life. When stressed, focus on the things that are within your control and take small, definitive steps to reduce the effects of stress on your mental health and well-being. By doing this, you're nudging your brain toward a more positive and resilient mindset.

- **Engage in activities and habits that make you feel good.** Engaging more often in activities you genuinely enjoy is an excellent way to boost positive thinking and develop resilience. In other words, do things that make you happy. Meditate, walk in nature, exercise, etc. Compliment a friend, loved one, classmate, or even a stranger. Do things that give you a sense of purpose and accomplishment. This will make each day meaningful and help you look forward to a future with meaning.

How to Build Resilience to Bounce Back from Setbacks and Failures

There are many ways to develop resilience to cope with stressful and difficult life events more effectively. No matter your chosen strategy, it begins with learning the 7 Cs of resilience, as published by the American Academy of Pediatrics. These seven qualities provide a roadmap for you to build resilience.

Here are the 7Cs of resilience:

1. **Competence:** a sense of being able to cope with stressful events and tough times

2. **Confidence:** a feeling of self-esteem and self-worth that pushes you to take risks and move forward to recover from setbacks

3. **Connection:** authentic and meaningful relationships with friends, family, and school or youth groups to create social support

4. **Character:** a desire to do the right thing, a sense of integrity, and the strength to follow through

5. **Contribution:** giving your time, talent, and caring to others, which has been shown to boost resilience and well-being while enhancing meaning

6. **Coping:** cultivating healthy and productive mechanisms to cope with stress rather than resorting to maladaptive habits

7. **Control:** a sense of responsibility for yourself and the decisions you make

With these in mind, here are seven approaches to help you build and develop resilience as you grow.

- **Make healthy lifestyle changes**

Practice being assertive and straightforward; learn to say "NO" to people who make unreasonable demands of you. Relax and take a few minutes daily to do things that calm you down, such as meditating, taking a bath, listening to music, or going for a walk alone or with your pet.

Explore new interests and hobbies, and dedicate appropriate time to them. Spend time with your family and friends, and take advantage of your social support network whenever you struggle.

Suppose you feel as if one aspect of your life is taking up all your time. In that case, make time for other equally important things. Maintain balance in your life.

- **Express how you feel**

You can benefit a lot from expressing what you're feeling. Talking about your emotions will serve you in different phases of your life. You might find it easy to express positive feelings such as joy and optimism—most people do. But it's just as important to notice and talk about your fears, anxiety, pain, and other unpleasant feelings. Remember that all emotions are normal and that the distress you get from negative emotions will pass. Teach yourself that it is OK to be sad.

- **Remind yourself of your strengths and amplify them**

A powerful way to build resilience is to identify and amplify your strengths. Find your unique talents and strengths, and learn how to use them skillfully to maneuver any situation you find yourself in. You will find them pretty handy when faced with challenges or setbacks.

- **Form healthy habits**

Engage in meditation, yoga, and other healthy habits. Eat wholesome food and spend time in nature. These activities support mental health and well-being. Incorporating these things in your life as early as possible ensures you continue them as you grow into adulthood.

- **Take care of your physical health**

Get enough sleep every night, and adopt healthier sleeping patterns. Become physically active if you aren't already, or intensify your present physical activities. In addition, exercise regularly and follow a healthy, balanced diet.

- **Practice mindfulness**

Mindfulness is the art of grounding yourself in the moment and paying attention to what's happening within and around you, all without judgment or criticism. Being mindful means staying in the present at all times.

Mindfulness is a skill that can teach you to regulate your emotions better and remain fully present in your experiences. You can practice mindfulness meditation to attune to your feelings and sensations and learn not to be overwhelmed.

By practicing this skill, you can teach your mind to notice your thoughts without engaging, judging, or reacting. This builds the strength and mental resilience that comes into play whenever you have a problem to solve or adversity to overcome.

- ## Don't be hard on yourself

Reward yourself when you accomplish set goals and praise yourself when necessary. Forgive yourself when you make mistakes or fail to achieve something you want. Remember that nobody is perfect, and ease up on yourself. Be easier on yourself and everyone around you.

Naturally, there will be times when you will struggle to cope with difficult situations. However, as you learn more about yourself and realize what you can or cannot manage, you will be able to personalize strategies to build your resilience, take difficulties in stride, and feel confident in your coping skills.

Remember that resilience-building is a process that won't just happen. But there is strength and courage in you that you don't know you have yet.

Step Five
Pump Up Your Self-Esteem

The teenage years are a "new environment" because you've never been here before. You're experiencing many changes and may struggle to maintain a physical and emotional balance.

You must have thought to yourself at some time, *If only I could be more confident. If only I could exhibit a little more boldness. If only I could believe in myself more.* Thankfully, you don't have to think too much because you are about to be all that and more.

Building and maintaining self-esteem can be challenging as a teen. It's even more difficult when you start a new school, be it high school or college. You find yourself in a new environment among people you've never been with, and it seems hard to keep your head up. You immediately lose what's left of the confidence you once had.

This chapter will walk you through how you can build your self-esteem. No matter where you are or what circumstance you're in, you can keep your head up and walk in confidence.

What It Means to Have Self-Esteem

You will better understand what it means to have self-esteem when you first know its definition. Self-esteem is the feeling of being confident in one's worth and abilities. It is the belief you have in yourself.

Simply put, self-esteem is how you value yourself. It is who you see if you look at yourself through other people's eyes. As you read these lines, think about it. What do you feel about yourself? Do you see any worth when you look at yourself in the mirror? Are you happy with the person you see on the other side? Whatever you see when you look at your reflection is your worth and, by extension, your self-esteem.

You are likely to have the following issues when you lack self-esteem.

- You will have a poor image of yourself.
- You will find it difficult to make friends.
- You will have trouble with your relationships.
- You may engage in early sexual activity, alcohol, or drugs to feel better.
- You will experience negative emotions like sadness, anxiousness, anger, and shame.
- You will experience low motivation in all you do.

But what can you gain from having self-esteem?

- Self-esteem helps you to act independent and mature. When you have self-esteem, you won't walk in other people's shadows. You won't be that friend who always has to tag along. You will be happy being yourself.

- Self-esteem helps you take pride in your achievements. It allows you not to be afraid to recognize it when you do well.

- Self-esteem helps you recognize areas where you need to improve yourself. It enables you to accept frustration and deal with it responsibly.

- Self-esteem makes you courageous to try new things and challenge yourself. It makes you believe that you can be and do anything.

- Self-esteem makes you realize you have the potential to help others with your abilities.

What can make you lose your self-esteem?

The situations you face and the people you interact with go a long way in determining how you feel about yourself. Below are some of the factors that can reduce your self-esteem.

- Friends with negative influence
- Uncaring parents, guardians, and other insensitive persons who influence your life
- Relocating or finding yourself in new or strange environments
- Unrealistic goals
- Trauma
- Abuse
- Prolonged illnesses
- Poor academic performance
- Negative emotions
- Loneliness

The 7 Components of Self-Esteem

1. Identity

Knowing your identity is the first component of self-esteem. And you can only find your sense of identity when you ask yourself, *Who am I?* Many people will quickly say they are doctors, attorneys, sisters, students, or daughters. These answers are labels people assign to themselves to describe who they are. With these labels, they can identify themselves in different contexts. For example, if I ask you who you are, you may say you are a student, a daughter, a granddaughter, and a choreographer. That's because, in different contexts, you can be described by those labels.

It's normal for people to identify more with a particular label, depending on where they find themselves. If you were in a school environment, you would most times describe yourself as a student, irrespective of the other things you are. There is nothing wrong with that. The problem is over-attaching yourself to a particular label and being overly emotional about it.

If you centered your life on being a "student," you will probably feel empty when you graduate. When asked who you are, referring to yourself as a student will be awkward because you're not. And because you were too emotionally attached to that label, you may feel as if nothing is left of you anymore. You will need help trying to rediscover who you are now, which is why we started this book by discussing the essence of self-discovery.

The best way to conquer this problem is to be involved in all aspects of your life. Build different interests and relationships and be actively engaged in them. As a student, remember to be a daughter, granddaughter, and choreographer rather than bury yourself in your academic pursuits alone. That way, your identity will be intact when your schooling ends. Your life will always have meaning because different groups in other places feel the impact of your existence. That's self-worth, and that's self-esteem.

2. Appreciation

This involves being grateful for the things you have, such as your strengths, relationships, potential, and accomplishments. People with low self-esteem typically see nothing good about themselves and cannot be grateful for much of anything.

As a teen, you have to value yourself. You can do this by being thankful for the things you can do. When was the last time you were grateful that others could smile because of you? That's a gift, and you should be thankful for it. Consider your various strengths and abilities and start expressing gratitude for them. Doing that will increase your self-esteem.

A gratitude journal is vital for increasing self-esteem because it can open your eyes to optimism through appreciating the positive things around you. While that is good, appreciation here as a component of self-esteem focuses on the good things within you. It helps you to enjoy being yourself and, as people will say, "be comfortable in your own skin." So, rather than dwell on those things you are yet to be, you should be thankful for those you are already.

3. Acceptance

Acceptance as a component of self-esteem is your ability to believe in yourself and accept yourself in a favorable light.

Have you ever noticed how some girls can never take a compliment in a good light? Someone tells them, "Your hair is beautiful." They respond by saying, "No, it's just there, nothing spectacular." That's low self-esteem speaking through them. Such responses come from mindsets of not being worthy or deserving of anything. And because of that mindset, they find it challenging to receive things from people. They cannot accept favors, compliments, or love from anyone. That in itself is against human nature. Humans are wired to give and receive love, so anything less than that is not normal.

It would help if you found yourself good enough to be applauded or complimented. So learn to accept it when it comes. Don't be afraid to be in the spotlight. When things like that happen, take it with a favorable disposition. Be proud of yourself for being worthy of being celebrated while staying modest enough to be objective about it.

4. Self-Confidence

You cannot talk about self-esteem without mentioning self-confidence. It is the belief you have in your competencies. It is when you know that "you can."

How would you feel if you were asked to solve an equation before the class, knowing fully well that you are knowledgeable in that topic? You'll approach the board with squared shoulders and your head high. Now, that's confidence. You trust your ability to solve the equation and arrive at the correct answer.

However, self-confidence doesn't always have to be the result of your knowing the answer to everything. It sometimes reflects your ability to learn even when you don't know the answers yet. That's because you recognize your capability to learn. You're not afraid of trying new things. You don't lose your peace when you go to a new environment because you trust your ability to adapt.

Self-confidence is being willing to take risks because you trust that you'll be fine and better at the end of the day. In your quest to succeed in all your life's endeavors, you may wait to achieve your goals, but self-confidence helps you stay patient and persistent. It enables you to realize that succeeding is not about "when" you succeed but "how" you stay focused and not give up on your dreams.

5. Pride

I know you're surprised, but there's a lot you need to learn about this component. Pride can be viewed from two perspectives.

There is unhealthy, negative pride and there is healthy, positive pride. Negative pride is when someone has an air of superiority over others. They feel they're better than everyone else. That's what you've always known about pride. Have you ever wondered why people exhibit this type of pride? Why does someone always feel threatened when others do well, and so they find a reason to act superior?

The truth is that such people have low self-esteem. They are afraid on the inside and always feel insecure. They have an unhealthy appetite for being in the spotlight. So, their only tactic for overcoming their fear and insecurity is forcing their supremacy on others. To make themselves appear better, they make others feel bad about themselves.

On the other hand, healthy pride is optimistic. It's a true sense of being worthy of admiration. Someone with healthy pride possesses self-respect and is always grateful for their abilities and accomplishments. Healthy pride is basking in your accomplishments and telling yourself with dignity, *I made it at last*. It isn't about putting anyone down; instead, it tells you to celebrate yourself and allow others to do so because you're worth celebrating.

6. Humility

Humility is not just about being unassuming. It can take a negative dimension if not appropriately handled. Just like pride, there is unhealthy and healthy humility. People with unhealthy humility lack self-worth and self-respect. They spend time dwelling on their mistakes and beating themselves up for past failures. They see only their shortcomings and are entirely blind to their abilities. It doesn't pay to have a mindset of being worthless and contemptible. It's very unhealthy and will only lead to more low self-esteem.

Healthy humility is not giving yourself more glory than is due. It is a state of being kind enough to value yourself and honest enough to improve on areas of your life that require it, while carefully drawing the line between humility and humiliation.

7. Selfishness

Selfishness as a component of self-esteem is not intended negatively. Put yourself first to build and maintain good self-esteem. That's because you need to be in your best state of health and have a good frame of mind and a healthy mindset before effectively impacting others with your strengths and abilities.

However, you must be careful not to be too selfish, which can make you arrogant and lose compassion for others. Being overly selfish also makes you feel unnecessarily entitled. On the other hand, if you practice "too little selfishness," meaning not putting yourself first as you should, you will end up hurting yourself. How? People will take undue advantage of you and take you for granted. You also lose out on deserved opportunities because you put others before yourself.

Strategies to Pump Up Your Self-Esteem

Use the following strategies to improve your self-esteem.

1. Identify your strengths

If you're going to improve how you feel about yourself, you must take time to identify your strengths, abilities, and potential. It will help if you make a list of these – as many as you can remember now – then keep updating as others come to mind. So, pick up a sheet of paper and begin to write. For clarity, I'll give you some examples of how you should write these attributes.

- *"I am beautiful."*
- *"I am intelligent."*
- *"I am a fast thinker."*
- *"I make the best pastries."*
- *"I am articulate."*
- *"I am resourceful."*
- *"I handle difficulties pretty well."*
- *"I am resilient."*

Go ahead and write a list that applies to you. Be honest as you write, and you'll be surprised at the many capabilities you possess. Next, after writing your list, place it somewhere you can see it every day. Your bathroom mirror is a perfect place to place it. The idea is to read your list out loud to yourself when you go in front of the mirror. As you do this repeatedly, your self-esteem will be pumped up daily as you begin to see a new you—the real you.

2. Practice self-love

You must love yourself first before seeing a difference in your self-esteem. Have you ever loved someone? A parent, a friend, or a boyfriend? Can you remember how you cared for those you loved and would have done anything to ensure they were happy? It would help if you did the same to yourself to increase your self-esteem. Show yourself kindness, tenderness, and affection. Treat yourself right, and within a short while, your perspective will change as you begin to place value on yourself.

3. Care for yourself

To increase your self-esteem, you must show great care for yourself. Take care of your health the best way you can. Eat right and ensure your body gets all the vital nutrients. Some teenage girls starve themselves whenever they're angry or sad. That's not right. You should eat regular meals so your body can be healthy. Also, maintain good hygiene. Bathe properly, care for your hair, wear clean clothes, and smell nice. It would help if you also got adequate sleep so your mind can stay sharp always. All these will increase your self-confidence when you're among your peers.

4. Stop comparing yourself with others

I'm not saying you shouldn't be challenged by other girls doing well in similar aspects. While that is good, you must not make other people your standard for success. Don't allow the performances of others to determine your happiness. Rather than making other people your standard, you should compare your current progress with your previous. Be your yardstick for measuring success.

5. Regulate social media use

As a young girl, you will see many things on social media that can influence how you perceive yourself. People are fond of putting up fake appearances on social media, which has led many teenage girls to see themselves as unworthy. Everyone always looks so "*beautiful*" and "*perfect*" online that you unconsciously make this your standard of how things should be. You must know that your role models online only allow you to see the aspect of themselves that helps them maintain their celebrity ratings. A closer look into their private lives will reveal the many issues they are saddled with that are unknown to the world.

To increase your self-esteem, you must find a way to regulate what you take from social media. While it can advance your learning and interactions, you must restrict any aspect that makes you lose your self-respect.

Are there people who make silly comments about you when you update your status or put up a picture of yourself? Those are cyberbullies, and there's only one thing you should do about them—block them! Don't allow anybody to make you feel bad about yourself. Anyone not contributing positively to your growth and happiness shouldn't be on your friend list.

6. Keep positive-minded friends

To a large extent, the kind of friends you keep will significantly influence how you feel about yourself. They can help to either increase or reduce your self-esteem. Take a close look at the people you have in your corner. Are they people with positive mindsets? Do they speak politely to others? Are they caring and compassionate? Do they encourage you to do better? Be quick to cut off any friend who teases you unnecessarily or sees only the worst in you. Surround yourself with friends who can build you up instead; that will change your self-esteem level for good.

7. Stop setting unrealistic goals

Stop setting goals that are impossible for you to achieve. You know your strengths and capabilities, so you should always set goals that you can attain for yourself. Unrealistic goals will only make you feel frustrated about yourself, and that will end up damaging your self-esteem. Once you strike all unrealistic goals off your list and choose to concentrate on those that are reasonable and attainable, your self-esteem will increase.

8. Help others

One quick way to pump up your self-esteem is to lend a helping hand to others. There are lots of people around you who need help in line with your abilities and strengths. Helping them makes you feel good about yourself. The look of satisfaction on their faces when you help them carry out a task or solve a problem is a sign that you are relevant.

9. Take photos of yourself

It has been proven that taking pictures of yourself often can improve how you see yourself. Start taking a picture of yourself more often, and soon you'll start admiring yourself.

10. Celebrate yourself

Be generous to yourself when you do well. When you get awarded, promoted, or recognized, you should be happy with your achievements and celebrate yourself.

And that's it for developing your self-esteem. The next chapter will focus on creating a rock-solid mindset to overcome challenges.

Step Six
Create a Rock-Solid Mindset

Are you familiar with the law of attraction? Let me give an example. Many teens struggle with confidence; they want success but lack the confidence to pursue their goals. An average teen might want to run a business or monetize a talent but fears failure. Unfortunately, the more you think of or talk about failing, the more likely you are to fail. Thinking about failure makes you attracted to it. This is why it is important to have a positive mindset and attitude.

Keeping a positive attitude when you're going through major transitions and changes can be tough. It is especially difficult for a teen, who has hardly any life experience. Find something to motivate you toward change to create a rock-solid, positive mindset.

Also, strive to be open-minded. In other words, see the world from varying perspectives and do your best to understand why people do certain things.

Positivity doesn't come easy to everyone. Sometimes, you need extra effort to push yourself to be positive. Life gets tough, and viewing things negatively is pretty automatic. But you mustn't allow negative thinking and energy to consume your life. Instead, challenge yourself to radiate positivity in everything you do. And that begins with creating a positive attitude toward life and its circumstances.

From learning who you are to worrying about fitting in and assuming new roles and responsibilities, your adolescent years won't be easy. In the face of these new challenges, you might find it hard to stay positive.

But, as I highlighted in Chapter Four, a positive mindset can help you to regulate your emotions, manage stress, improve your health, increase your resilience, and boost your chances of overcoming adversities and meeting your goals.

The Power of Positive Thinking

Nowadays, you probably see positive thinking everywhere you go in the form of vision boards, manifestation, positive affirmations, and phrases such as "No bad days." It is almost like everyone on earth wants to harness the power of positive thinking. I wouldn't be wrong to say there is a proliferation of positivity.

Unfortunately, many people really don't know what it means to think positively. They believe it is about living a life of rainbows and sunshine and staying away from negativity, but I'm afraid that's not quite accurate.

Our thoughts indeed dictate our feelings and actions. And our actions, in turn, dictate our success in life in our relationships, career, and other aspects. Our thoughts also play a vital role in forming our values and beliefs, which affects how we perceive the world and the quality of our interpersonal relationships.

With the emphasis on positive thinking today, it is easy to get caught up in only thinking and feeling positively. To build a fulfilling life, you must stop masking the weeds in the garden of your mind with positive thinking and learn to pluck them out instead.

The best approach is to cultivate an overall mental attitude that embraces positive and negative emotions and knows how to control them. In essence, you must learn to get to the root of your problems instead of trying to override them with positive thinking.

The benefits of creating a positive mindset are infinite. Living life with a negative mindset will only attract negative outcomes in your life.

When going through a tough time, it's easy to shut out the world. You go through life aimlessly, not particularly interested in anything around you. A positive mindset imbues you with energy, which makes you remain aware of your environment.

Cultivating a positive mental attitude makes you increasingly self-aware, alert, and sensitive to the feelings and needs of people around you.

One of the perks of creating a positive mindset is increased productivity. Positivity stimulates the brain to function at optimal levels. It also boosts your energy levels, making you better charged to complete tasks and pursue your goals. This can be helpful in your daily life as it enables you to accomplish your goals more quickly.

Adopting a positive attitude can also influence people to offer their cooperation. For example, suppose you have a huge class project due, and you want a classmate to help. In that case, they would be more inclined to help if you're radiating positive energy, which is generally more attractive to people. On the other hand, if they are repelled by negative energy, they will be less likely to assist you in completing the project.

Another benefit of creating a positive mindset is that it enhances your problem-solving skills. Problem-solving requires viewing an issue from different perspectives and devising different tactics to arrive at a solution.

A study by The National Center for Biotechnology Information found that participants who watched a positive video before completing a task were more inclined to problem-solving and performed better than those who watched a depressing video.

This study highlights how positive energy can positively impact our ability to tackle challenging situations and complete our tasks.

How often do you regret not doing something you wanted to do? Teenagers often shy away from doing things they want because they fear making mistakes. If you struggle with this fear, cultivating a positive attitude can help you overcome it.

A positive mindset tells you that you can achieve anything you set your mind to and shows you how valuable you are. As I said, a positive mindset will boost your productivity. This means you'll start achieving your everyday goals, boosting your confidence and encouraging you to pursue bigger goals.

In the words of Ryan C. Lowe, "It is up to you to choose every day to get off your attitude and to create a positive lifestyle for yourself."

Positive thinking is seeing the good in a situation instead of expecting the worst. It's a mental attitude that encourages you to anticipate happiness, success, and productivity. It leverages the law of attraction to create a positive feedback loop that attracts more and more good into your life.

However, this doesn't mean positive thinking is a cure-all for a happy and fulfilling life. It is not an automatic solution to deep-seated negative beliefs and fears. And it isn't about telling yourself to be happy no matter the situation.

Mastering positive and negative emotions is the key to creating a fulfilling life. Positive thinking is only one of the tools you can use to achieve this.

The power of positive thinking is incredible. The idea that our minds can change our world may seem too good to be true, but it is. I have witnessed and experienced in my own life how forging a positive mindset can transform a person's life.

Positive thinking means you seek solutions and anticipate finding them. You don't ignore your problems; rather than complain about them or let them overwhelm you, you actively seek solutions to overcome them.

It means you take charge of your life consistently because you realize you're now at a phase where you're in direct control of your life's progression.

Positive thinkers look for the bright sides of challenges and expect to work them out. If you've ever listened to a speech on the impact of positive thinking, you've most likely experienced that familiar rush that comes with it. That alone is a testament to the power of positive thinking.

Cultivating a positive attitude means you have an optimistic outlook, and that indicates hope. You expect things to work out and believe you will be successful. You are confident and believe you will overcome any adversity, obstacle, or setback.

Here are some benefits of positive thinking and how it contributes to developing a positive mindset.

- Positive thinking creates a positive mental attitude, improving all life areas.

- It improves physical and mental well-being.

- It decreases stress and anxiety and lowers the risk of depression.

- It increases confidence and optimism, which boosts your overall outlook.

- Such a mental state boosts your optimism, which improves your relationship with others.

- This mental attitude motivates you to improve your life and those around you.

- It substitutes negative self-talk with positive self-talking, which boosts your self-esteem and confidence.

When you cultivate a habit of thinking positively, you're better equipped to cope with stress, anxiety, and life's challenges. This enhances your problem-solving skills and makes you think more creatively.

Positive thinking improves your mood and helps you form healthier and more meaningful relationships with family, friends, peers, and new acquaintances.

As anyone does, you can choose to either allow negative thoughts to control you or else think positively. But remember that cultivating a habit of thinking positively will unlock many benefits—internal peace, happiness and contentment with self, better health, improved relationships, and overall satisfaction.

So, how do you increase your tendency toward positive thinking?

Tips to Nurture Positive Thoughts

Positive thinking isn't a magical exercise that will make all your problems disappear. But it will make them appear more manageable and help you take a more productive and healthy approach to hardship. You can nurture positive thinking through a few strategies proven effective by science, including positive imagery and positive self-talk.

Here are a few tips and strategies to get you started on training your brain to think positively.

- **Focus on the good things**

Challenges and adversities are a part of life. When faced with an obstacle or setback, focus on the good things, no matter how insignificant they seem. Look for the proverbial silver lining in the cloud. You will most likely find it, although that may not happen immediately.

For example, if a friend cancels plans with you, don't think beyond what they tell you about why they canceled. Instead, focus on how you now have free time to catch up on an entertaining TV show or some other activity you like.

- **Practice positive self-talk**

We're hardwired to be our own worst critics. As a result, we're usually harder on ourselves than we are on others. Over time, this can create a negative feedback loop in which you have the worst opinions of yourself. This can be hard to shake or get rid of.

To get out of the loop, you must be mindful of the voice in your head and counter its negative messages with positive self-talk. Changing how you talk to yourself can boost your ability to cope with stress and regulate your feelings and behaviors.

- **Identify negative areas**

What areas of your life are you most negative about? Examine the different aspects of your life and identify the ones filled with negativity. If you aren't sure, speak to a trusted friend or peer. You can also talk to your parents. Chances are, any of these people will have some insight you will find remarkably helpful.

Once you identify these areas, tackling them one by one becomes considerably easier.

- **Keep a gratitude journal**

Gratitude has been shown to decrease stress, boost self-esteem, and nurture resilience in difficult times. Each day, think of a person, thing, or moment that brought you happiness or comfort and express gratitude for them. Thank a classmate for assisting with a project, your parent for doing the dishes, or your puppy for her unconditional love.

Writing down things you're grateful for is even more beneficial than expressing your gratitude orally. Keeping a gratitude journal can improve your optimism, outlook, and well-being.

- **Surround yourself with positive people**

Negativity is contagious, and so is positivity. Think of the people with whom you spend the most time. Pay attention to how someone with a bad "vibe" can bring down the mood of everyone else around them. Positive people have the opposite effect on people around them.

Studies have shown that spending time around positive people can improve self-esteem and make you more likely to reach your goals. With this in mind, surround yourself with friends and peers who lift you and encourage you to see the brighter side of any situation.

- **Open yourself up to humor**

Laughter reduces symptoms of stress, anxiety, and depression. It enhances mood, self-esteem, and coping skills. Open yourself up to humor in all situations, especially difficult ones. Allow yourself to laugh no matter how hard things may seem. It will instantly brighten your mood and make the situation seem a little less serious.

Pretending or forcing yourself to laugh even when you don't feel like it can instantly lighten your mood and lower stress.

- **Start each day on a positive note**

Create a ritual to help you start daily on a positive and uplifting note. For example, before you leave the house, tell yourself it will be a great day. You can also listen to an upbeat song or podcast. Another way is to compliment or do something nice for another person.

How do you think positively when times are hard?

Thinking positively when in serious distress, grieving, or tackling a difficult problem is one of the most challenging things you'll ever have to do. During this time, don't be fixated on finding the silver lining. Instead, channel your energy into connecting with your support network.

Again, positive thinking isn't about suppressing, ignoring, or avoiding negative thoughts and feelings. You may be surprised to learn that the lowest points in our lives often inspire us to make positive changes.

Treat yourself like a good friend who needs support and comfort when going through a difficult time. What would you say to a friend in a similar situation? You'd likely acknowledge and validate their feelings and then offer support by gently reminding them that things will improve.

The more you practice, the more you'll learn to approach things with a positive attitude and outlook.

How to Develop a Positive Mental Attitude

A positive mental attitude can help you remain strong and confident. A positive mental attitude ensures you don't succumb to negative thinking and emotions or react emotionally to situations.

By cultivating a positive mindset, you learn to let things roll off your back, approach situations with a smile, and find joy in the happy occurrences in your life.

Here are seven steps to help you develop a positive mental attitude.

1. **Like yourself.** Change how you feel about yourself by viewing your environment positively. Be confident and proud of yourself. Take care of your needs and every area of your life. Remember that you're a wonderful person and deserve wonderful things in life.

2. **Don't take things personally.** Your opinion about yourself should be the most important thing to you. Words can't impact your feelings if you don't let them. If someone says something rude to you, smile politely and walk away. Not only will this make you feel better, but it will help you avoid unwanted mess.

3. **Be kind to everyone.** Everyone is on a journey to build a positive, fulfilling life in their own way. Be kind to everyone around you; seeing them smile will make your heart lighter and happier. A positive outlook on your emotions and actions is a step in the right direction.

4. **Empower yourself.** It helps to remind yourself that you're powerful from time to time. Being a teen means you probably have only a slight idea of what you should be doing, so you tend to conform to your external environment. You play roles and identify with certain things that end up defining who you think you are. But the truth is, you are none of these things. You are more than any label. You are not your thoughts, feelings, or circumstance. What you are is far greater than what your mind tries to define you. This is why you are more powerful than you think you are. So, learn to embrace your inner power.

5. **Take control of your physical and mental state.** It reflects in our body language when we're having a bad day. Have you noticed that when you're having a not-so-good day, you slump, avoid eye contact with others, and cross your arms when you feel uncomfortable? You also stop being aware of your environment and cede control to your circumstance. This isn't empowering. Negative body language creates a negative feedback loop, reinforcing your unhealthy mindset.

   Positive thinking is about the body as much as it is about the mind. Take control of your physiology by maintaining a power pose to keep you feeling strong and positive. If you do this, people around you will perceive and return the same energy you're radiating.

6. **Form new habits.** Developing a positive mental attitude is impossible without letting go of unhelpful habits and forming new ones. Do not let yourself get caught up in negative thinking patterns. Refocus your energy and form new, empowering habits that foster positive thinking.

7. **Choose your words carefully.** Transforming how you talk to yourself is key to creating a positive mindset. The words you use both in your mind and conversations impact your mindset. Positive self-talk can improve your mental state, help with emotional regulation, and more. Pay attention to how you label and describe yourself and your emotions.

   You may find it helpful to write down negative words you use throughout the day. For every negative word, write down a positive alternative. Practice using the alternatives in your interactions with yourself and others.

   This can be overwhelming, so start with just one area of your life where negative thoughts are prevalent. Stay aware, so you can catch yourself in those moments and address them instantly. Then, work your way up from there.

How to Engage in Positive Self-Talk

You mentally talk to yourself all the time. You give yourself more feedback than anyone else could. Self-talk can affect all areas of your life, whether negative or positive. Negative self-talk is unhealthy and discouraging. Examples include:

- *"I'm stupid."*
- *"I'm not good at this."*
- *"I can't do it."*

In contrast, positive self-talk is inspiring and encouraging. It pushes you to pursue and achieve your goals. Examples of positive self-talk include:

- *"I am good enough."*
- *"I can do it."*
- *"If I work hard, I can."*

Self-talk is powerful. Positive self-talk sends the same chemical messages as having a positive experience sends to your brain. Yet, so does negative self-talk. Your mind believes the conversations that happen in your head.

If you tell yourself, *"I am bad at making new friends. I always end up looking stupid,"* you will experience certain physiological changes such as shallow breathing, increased heart rate, tightening stomach, etc. This is how negative self-talk impacts the body and mind.

You can talk yourself into or out of anything. Often, we aren't aware of the things we say to ourselves. So, the first step in engaging in positive self-talk is to pay attention to what you say to yourself.

To engage in positive self-talk:

- Focus on how you want things to be. Choose your words carefully. Phrase your statements in the present, even if they haven't happened yet. For example, don't say, "I will be a terrific friend." Say, "I am a terrific friend."

- When you think negatively or blame yourself for things out of your control, ask yourself if the thought is true. Find proof to support or disprove the thought. Then, replace it with a true statement that is also positive.

- Ask your loved ones to call you out when you make a negative statement. And when they do, switch to positive self-talk immediately.

- Embrace your mistakes and accept setbacks as an inevitable part of life. Tell yourself that mistakes happen to teach us a lesson. You're capable of rising above your mistakes and moving forward.

- Find solutions instead of focusing on a problem. Rather than complain about what you cannot do, focus on what you can do.
- Reduce your usage of words like "never" and "always." Often, these words make things sound worse than they are.
- Swap criticism for praise. Be your own number-one fan. Praise yourself and take credit when you do something well.

Here's a list of affirmations to help you practice positive self-talk. You can choose from this list or create personalized affirmations.

- *I am enough.*
- *I am amazing.*
- *My challenges help me grow.*
- *I can find solutions to all of my problems.*
- *My mistakes are opportunities for me to grow and learn.*
- *I am confident and courageous.*
- *I control my own happiness.*
- *I can make a difference.*
- *I am worthy of love.*
- *There is no one better to be than me.*
- *Good things are coming my way.*
- *I matter.*
- *I choose to think and feel positive today.*
- *I can do anything I set my mind on.*
- *I can be anything I want.*
- *I accept who I am.*

- *I am going to have a wholesome day.*
- *I am capable of so much.*
- *My friends love and respect me.*
- *I will walk through my fears.*
- *Everything will be okay.*
- *I can do better next time.*

Remember that the ultimate goal is to use positive self-talk to strengthen self-confidence and create a positive mindset. This will help you achieve independence and reach your potential as you transition from adolescence to adulthood.

Step Seven
Find a Balance

As a teenager, you are expected to be many things at the same time: a child to your parent/guardian, a sibling, a student in your school, a friend to your peers, a special person to someone, a member of a club or other social activity you are part of.

Sometimes, you get overwhelmed by the series of adventures you and your friends have created, and sometimes you get drowned by dramas happening in your life. Sometimes, you are engaging in activities that bring income. And when you add all of these together, the life of an average teenager can be overwhelmingly challenging.

The pressure of responsibilities placed upon you can be daunting. Meanwhile, your teenage life is meant to shape your future. Therefore, finding a balance at this stage is crucial to shaping your future. As much as you don't want to end up lazy, you also want to avoid ending up focusing too much on work or school to the extent that you have no social life or even time to breathe.

But the problem, as always, is how to find that balance. How do you understand your life's complexities and make it appear simple? How do you even set priorities in your confusion? How do you set realistic goals? How can you define what goals to accomplish at a certain time? What should come first, or what should have top priority? And most of all, how do you take care of yourself?

At this stage, you have to take charge of your life. This is the time to define your priorities and be sincere about what you want out of life. It does not have to be something conventional, but it should be something you are passionate about—something valid.

For instance, you cannot aspire to be a cybercriminal—it isn't valid because if you have to think about when you get caught, that would be a public shame; every bit of your time and energy spent on being that kind of person will go down the drain with a jail sentence. So, you must always consider the end game of every aspiration. If it appears negative, that clearly indicates that such an aspiration is invalid.

But when you find that good person you want to become, it becomes easier to talk about setting priorities or how to channel your energy and focus on achieving that personality while maintaining a healthy social interaction with your environment. The key is finding a balance.

Balancing Life and School – How to Juggle It All

Social interaction, school life, life goals, peer adventure, family—these only partially capture the number of issues you need to juggle daily. Life expects you to find a balance in the face of these typical interactions that spark different emotions. The responsibility of finding a balance is solely on you, but you can find your balance by following the tips below:

1. Define your priority

The first place to start is to define your priorities. Stay calm and clear from the thoughts of your life's priority. You should know what you want your future life to look like. However, if you find it daunting to decide what you want to be or what you like the most, you can start by learning how to define your priority daily.

On a typical day, you must go to school and return home to do some home chores, hang out with your friends, engage in your school projects, etc. What you should do when you have so much to do in a day is to define what's most important to you.

2. Have one goal at a time

The next thing is to set a goal. You'll be doing a lot of damage if you set too many goals for yourself. For instance, if you have school projects or extra-curricular activities to accomplish, plan on accomplishing only some things on a day that may be counterproductive. You may set a goal to accomplish a particular task each day. For example, you have three projects to submit at school and must engage in your extra-curricular activities. In this scenario, you should spread the accomplishment of those projects across the days of the week. And then, if your practices are rigorous, you can engage on days when you don't have the task of working on a school project.

The bottom line is you should try to accomplish only a few things at a time, especially because you may end up doing nothing or burn out easily, making you unable to accomplish other goals afterward.

3. Learn effective allocation of time

Time allocation is something you have to work on deliberately. Otherwise, you may need help finding that balance. There are just 24 hours a day, enough to work, play and rest. All you need is to learn time management.

Now, you should avoid spending all your time on schoolwork—there wouldn't be a balance. Neither should you spend your entire time with your extra-curricular activities, as that would also mean an imbalance in your work-school-home-social life. Therefore, allocate time in a way that balances your life. Take note of your priority for the day in that time allocation.

You must follow through with your plan when you allocate your time properly. If you are faced with a difficult task at a particular time allocated to it, you should quickly find help from a friend, teacher, or guardian.

Don't find reasons to procrastinate. Also, avoid impromptu situations that might disrupt your schedule for the day, but if there is an impromptu situation, there is no problem with disruption every once in a while.

4. Make it easy on yourself

Learn how to take it easy. Know that certain situations are unavoidable. Finding that school-home-work-social life is an ongoing event. So, think of it as a one-step-at-a-time process and learn how to adjust whenever unforeseen circumstances surface.

When you set a realistic schedule instead of a perfect one, it makes it easier to adjust and consistently accomplish your daily goals.

5. Know your limit when multitasking

I know how important multitasking is for you to accomplish some important goals. However, if you can avoid multitasking, by all means, avoid it. Multitasking drains your energy and makes you spend more time on each task than you would have if you handled the tasks individually.

When you have more than one must-do task, taking them one at a time will lead to accomplishing something. If you try to do too much, it can lead to depression, which arises when you start seeing yourself as a failure.

In the face of numerous must-dos, vet them and sort out the most important. Focus on your most important tasks, and you can move to the next task when you are done. If you find yourself completing the tasks, pat yourself on the shoulder. If you don't, you are still good at what you do and can give yourself a pat on the shoulder with a promise to do better the next day.

6. Take care of yourself

Taking care of yourself requires paying attention to and respecting your body. Be conscious of how your schedule affects your mental and emotional health. You also need to ensure you are not cheating yourself out of finding time to relax and have fun.

You need to sleep adequately, especially if school tasks and assignments are highly demanding. Sleeping helps your brain and physical body relax, which is also important for mental health.

Taking care of yourself also includes spending time with family and friends. It includes engaging in recreational activities such as golfing, swimming, dancing, etc.

How to Strike the Right Balance Between Responsibilities and Relaxation

Now that you can juggle your work-school-home-social life, you are faced with finding the balance between responsibilities and relaxation. This is the core of finding balance because you can't afford to keep working and working, moving relentlessly from one task to another. It will be easy to burn out quickly, leaving you tired, confused, and clueless about where to start.

Therefore, finding peace, enjoying rest, and having fun are important. You can strike that balance if you can answer these four fundamental questions:

1. What does prioritizing mean to you?

This is necessarily the first question because the answer opens the door to finding that balance. When you hear of prioritizing, the thing that comes to mind is arranging your tasks according to their importance. With this, you begin to prioritize only one aspect of your life that you feel is important to you. For example, you may become preoccupied with the school aspect of your life while the other aspects become redundant.

This strategy of prioritizing is counterproductive. At the end of the day, you'll burn out because, at that point, you'll be faced with stress, doubts about your ability, and confusion concerning the usefulness of prioritization itself.

When prioritizing, consider *every* aspect of your life. This includes your most important school task, social activity, house chore, friend, etc. Leaving no aspect behind gives you a balanced life.

To feel safe, you should create time for *each* aspect of your life, prioritizing the most time to the most important aspect. These don't necessarily have to fit into your 24 hours. You can create a weekly or monthly agenda to fit your home-work-social-school life, the aim being to ensure you strike a balance.

2. What is the work-school-home-social life balance to you?

The next question is, what does it mean to balance all the aspects of your life? Now you wonder if that is even possible. First, no one's definition of balance can fit yours. This is because you are unique and, by implication, have unique goals. What makes you happy and keeps you going can be different from that of others.

Happiness lies in the source of strength, so if you can allocate time to what makes you happiest, that gives you renewed energy to pursue who you want to be. Those activities that are your least priority are still important—spending time with friends, going for an afternoon walk, going to a concert or watching a movie, etc. Constant interaction with the immediate environment usually gives you a sense of belonging. For instance, do things with your friends, go for a weekend picnic, show up for a family getaway, be part of a social event, etc.

While balance for you may mean more social life, it may mean more school life for others. It could mean more work-life for someone else. It will ultimately be defined by you and does not mean giving all aspects of your life an equal share of your attention. How much time you allot to an aspect of your life depends largely on its contribution to your mental health. For instance, you'll want less time with your family if you come from a toxic home. On the other hand, if your social or extra-curricular activity gives you so much energy, you should give more time to that.

3. What do you do with your time?

What do you do with your time in a month? What's the ratio of achievement to the time put in? What are the things you spend the most time on? Do you feel more fulfilled after spending more time on those things? Do you feel like you wasted so much time? Why?

These questions are necessary to help audit your time and what you spend most of your time on. It will immediately show you whether you are on the right path. It guards against wasting your time doing nothing or excessively engaging in only one aspect of your life and disregarding the other.

After answering those questions, you can make the necessary adjustments to find a balance. You can then create a monthly schedule to fit all aspects of your life. Allot time based on an activity's social or intellectual importance.

Create a weekly schedule to further break down your activities, setting milestones for yourself. After that, you can create a daily schedule for yourself. This way, your 24 hours are properly accountable, and this does not imply that it is full of different activities. It could be one activity added to your normal daily routine.

4. How do you set time boundaries?

Have you ever set a time-bound activity before? Were you able to stick to the plan, or did you fail? Setting time-bound activities ensures that you find that balance. There are 24 hours in a day, which could be too much time or too little for your daily tasks to be achieved. It's so easy to waste time doing nothing or spend so much time doing something that you don't even need to do.

A practical example is spending hours chatting with a friend, probably gossiping. When this is happening in your free time or the time scheduled for such interaction, it's okay. But if it's happening at the time scheduled for your school project, that's not okay.

So, when setting a schedule for the day, make sure the tasks are time-bound. It would be smart to list several things to do and mark the time they'll be done during the day. This can prevent you from over-studying, and it can also prevent you from spending too much time with your friends when there are other things to be done.

It's important to create a time limit for each activity to save time and consequently leave out the other agenda for the day. If you set an hour for study, that time limit helps you stick to the plan and gives you space for the other activities of the day.

Maximizing your daily schedule requires more than just the commitment to balance your life's aspects. It takes discipline to help you stick to whatever plan you create. If you find it difficult to follow through on your schedules because of distractions, you can find an accountability partner—a friend or family member that will ensure that you're sticking to your plan for the day.

Coping with Stress

You may inevitably still get stressed out or mentally drained, even with good time management. It's a lot of mental assertion to walk through a day with many schedules and a time lag. School projects, extra-curricular activities, and sometimes working can cause you to get overwhelmed.

If you constantly subdue your body under stress, your body's functionality will decline. This is when you realize that you get tired easily and don't find as much excitement as you used to get with the things you love doing. When you reach this point, understand that your body is stressed.

It becomes complicated when you start seeing some of the symptoms below:

- Poor sleep over time
- Poor concentration
- Need for the use of drugs and alcohol
- Severe headaches
- Being irritable and easily angered

While these problems are predominant among teenagers who are exposed to illegal drugs and alcohol, sometimes a normal teenager may feel stressed, which usually depends on the nature of school/work/home life as well. Stress is also common for teenagers from a toxic home or environment.

You can deal with stress and maintain your balance with a positive mindset. With positivity, you can deal with stress in the following ways:

1. Find your balance

The very fact that you are feeling stressed means that your schedule needs to be balanced. You know, sometimes we feel that school is more important, then we dedicate a lot more time to it than the other aspects of our lives. Meanwhile, school is brain-tasking and, depending on the demands of your course of study, requires a lot from you. This is why you should also be able to create as much time for fun activities.

Think about the fun that excites you, such as gardening, swimming, etc. Also, review the number of hours you spend sleeping. Ideally, the body needs at least eight hours of sleep, so you should leave at least that much time for it in your schedule.

Exercise is a daily routine that can help you find balance in your work-school-home-social life. Exercise eases stress because it increases blood circulation and flushes out stress hormones.

Finding your balance may mean taking a break such as, say, a short vacation. You leave your school and work life behind during the break.

2. Stay away from stimulants

Caffeine, nicotine, codeine, and other stimulants have a huge negative impact on the body. Avoid starting your day with caffeine. Use exercise as a stimulant for alertness and energy. Also, stay away from alcohol as much as possible, especially when trying to relieve your body from stressors.

3. Find support

When stressed, the best thing for you is to have someone to talk to. Ideally, it would help if you had someone with much experience – such as an adult – because they have passed through the stage themselves and can understand what you are going through. If you have a supportive parent or guardian, you should take advantage of their encouragement. However, you can also seek professional help if you cannot find the positive energy required.

Finding a balance is very fundamental to healthy living. Therefore, by all means, strive for that balance.

Step Eight
Create the Life You Love

Living the life you love is more than wishful thinking. The world is full of distractions, with many people trying to define what a good life is all about. You'll meet with people who'll tell you what you should do or try to sell their dreams to you. You are better off when you can decide who you are and want to be. That way, you can champion creating the life you love.

A whole world is trying to create a life for you, but it may never be able to create the life you love. There are so many negative people, some of whom aren't even aware that they give off some negative energy. You also have social media to deal with; social media has become a major influencing platform. You must learn to purge yourself or define your life to avoid consuming too much negativity without realizing it.

Let's take a look at some of the practical ways to create the life you'll love.

Get Rid of Negativity

Negativity is that opportunistic pest that feeds on your self-esteem. If you let it, it will keep feeding until all your confidence, sense of self-worth, and self-esteem are gone. It will leave you feeling inadequate; you'll never feel good or worthy enough.

You are good, beautiful, smart, and perfect enough for anyone. But it would help if you shut out the voices questioning your abilities or making you feel like you don't measure up to societal standards. Whether it is a voice from within or a person you relate with, you can shut out their negativity and start to pursue the life you love.

Negativity has a way of affecting your physical health. So, you need to eliminate it no matter how hard that is, especially when dealing with someone you love or who is close to you.

Some of the ways to get rid of negativity are:

- **Be grateful**

One way to successfully eliminate negativity from the thoughts inside your head is to learn gratitude. There is no way you'll find nothing to be thankful for because, for all it's worth, you are still alive. There is always hope for a better tomorrow.

- **Build emotional resilience**

To get rid of external negativity is to build emotional resilience. This helps you take charge of your life to the point that you have total control over your emotional responses to negativity.

- **Practice self-honesty**

Tell yourself the truth at all times. You may not be as tall as others, but you are not as tall because you don't need to be. That doesn't define your intelligence or your inner beauty.

On the other hand, when you are being given some dose of negativity by others, be honest about it. For instance, does it hurt? Does it make you feel less than yourself? If you answer yes, then it's time to let those people know. Nothing is more important than your happiness in life. So don't make excuses for anyone. Analyze the situation and let them know.

- **Create boundaries**

If you allow people to taunt you, they will continue to do that. But you can create a threshold of healthy relationship/ interaction/communication. Once that threshold is crossed, it's time to say goodbye to the friendship. Always make your friends understand that a toxic attitude is no longer tolerated.

- **Let it go**

Don't beat yourself up because of how another person disrespects or treats you. The action of another person toward you is solely on them. Most times, there's no way you can change them. The only fixing that needs to be done is your self-esteem. Rather than dwell on why they were negative toward you, you can ensure their actions do not affect you. Let go of the feeling of perfection and accept who you are and the way you are.

- **Be a positive person**

You also have to be a positive person. Talk positively at all times about yourself and others. Don't be caught gossiping about another person or telling lies about another person. Always treat people the way you want to be treated.

Social Media Cleanse

Social media is now a major influencing platform. You have lots of negativity and content, defining social standards and subtly reminding you why you'll never be good enough. The worst is when you try to conform to the standards and then begin to hate how you look or are. Afterward, you'll begin to try out a lot of unhealthy practices to help you conform to someone you are not.

If you've gotten to that point where you are completely overtaken by social media content, it is time to purge yourself of the negative information or perception. To purge yourself, you can follow the steps below:

- **Own your social media feed**

The truth is you own your social media feed. Be deliberate about owning your feed and permit only content that satisfies your positivity standards. This means that you should unfollow negative people and block harmful content. Get rid of all negativity, no matter how subtle. For instance, if you are a plus-size person, you should avoid feeds that are mainly about slim or curvy girls. You can explore a lot of content in the plus-size category.

- **Find your community**

Join groups that align with your personality and belief system. There's no need to join a group just because you want to be the antagonist or try to prove a point. That's an example of giving negative energy that will most likely be reciprocated. There's certainly your kind of person out there with your belief system. Find them.

- **Know when to stop**

If you go on endlessly on social media, surfing from one platform to another, it'll always have negative repercussions. Don't be online all day. Most importantly, you must know when to stop. You don't need to be worried about who must have texted you or what is trending next. You don't owe anyone a 24-hour online presence, so learn to limit your hours spent on social media.

You can set time limits on your apps. Also, you can stay away from a platform periodically. Surely you had a life before these platforms, so you can definitely do without them for a week or so.

Create a Healthy Day

The journey of creating a life you love starts with how you spend your day. It starts with each step you take toward making the best of your interaction with your environment. So, every single day, try to create a memorable experience just for you. It begins with a healthy day, and a typical healthy day follows this pattern:

- **Create your day**

See each day as a journey. Planning your journey before embarking on it makes sense. Schedule the activities for the day so that you can tell if it will be a good or bad day even before your day starts. Give allowance for a Plan B or a Plan C in your schedule. Sometimes, things don't go as we planned. For such instances, your second or third line of action puts you on the safer side to keep your good day going.

However, have a resolution right from the beginning of your day:

- You are going to have a good day.
- Nothing will stop you from doing one good thing.
- You'll stick to your schedules unless a circumstance makes it impossible.

● **Learn something new**

The world is full of discoveries and enough to keep you busy for the rest of your life. When you set your mind to learning, you set yourself up for an adventure for the day. That way, your mind is in tune with paying attention to details because you want to be able to come up with something new you learned for the day.

Meanwhile, when setting yourself up for this adventure, ensure that your focus is on positivity. You want to learn something positive and unlearn something negative as well. It could be a nice short quote that resonates with you. It could be a passing comment. It could be something you learned about the world. Just ensure it is something positive about the world or life.

● **Reflect on your day**

Find time to reflect on your day at the end of each day. List your goals for the day and the things you were able to achieve. List the number of things you learned that day.

The purpose of self-reflection is not to scold or rebuke yourself for your shortcomings—that would be a negative energy. Rather, you should reflect on all of the things you could achieve and all the things you couldn't achieve. Reflect on the possible reason you could not achieve some of your goals.

Sometimes, you assign tasks that are more than your capacity to carry out. For instance, if you cannot keep up with your goals for at least five days in a row, it means that your schedule could be beyond your capacity or that the goals are not things you are passionate about.

Most importantly, reflection does not mean you should be hard on yourself.

Engage in Physical Exercise

Starting your day with some aerobics routine or exercises that strengthen your cardiovascular muscle is a great day to start a day. Exercise helps to build mental capacity and also helps maintain healthy self-esteem.

Some of the benefits of engaging in physical exercise:

- **It increases your self-esteem**

It starts with your ability to be consistent with your daily routine. It takes endurance to keep pushing yourself each day. If you succeed by pushing yourself daily, it gives you a sense of accomplishment. It also helps you lose some weight and increases your muscle tone. Aerobics helps define your curves. The more you see this improvement, the more you feel a sense of worth that boosts your self-esteem.

- **It's a brain booster**

Exercises are great brain boosters; this is why it is encouraged that you start your day with some physical exercises. It helps strengthen your memory and builds your intelligence. According to studies on the effect of cardiovascular exercises on humans, it was discovered that exercises such as walking or jogging initiate a process known as neurogenesis. Neurogenesis is the process of creating new brain cells. It strengthens the hippocampus, the part of the brain that retains memory and new learning. It also helps your creative ability and mental alertness. All you have to do to start your day is take a good walk, jog, or run.

- **It helps fight depression**

Scientifically, exercise increases the endorphin level, which is the chemical that produces the feeling of happiness in the body. This is why doctors recommend mild physical exercise to fight against some heart-related diseases. When more endorphins are released into your system, there's automatically no room for depression. Your stress levels will also be reduced.

Exercise stimulates norepinephrine production, improving your cognitive ability and thinking. When you exercise, you will be in a better position than a person without physical exercise to respond positively to stressful situations.

- **It affords a better night's rest**

Try exercising the next day if you have trouble getting a good night's rest or a day's nap. The increased temperature from that continuous exercise can calm the mind. However, the exercises are best in the morning to start your day. According to experts, exercising before bedtime is counter-effective.

Use Affirmations

Affirmations are statements we utter to tell our minds and brains to work toward confirming the statements we make. They are not magical words that immediately start fixing your life how you want it to be. Rather they are a propellant for your success. So, nothing will change if you only want to say some positive things to yourself and go to bed.

Here's how it works:
The brain can't tell the difference between reality and imagination. This is why when you pretend to laugh and continue to do that, you either find something really funny or find your unnecessary laughter funny. Try it.

Therefore, when you say affirmative words, you are fueling your brain because it will activate your body to work toward achieving the statements you have made.

Neuroplasticity is the brain's ability to change accordingly or adapt as a response to growth or reorganization. Affirmations help you create a mental image where you see yourself achieving what you say about yourself. For instance, you might be anxious about a test. Still, when you keep telling yourself, *I got this; I'm going to be fine*, and you repeat this even in your anxiety, you'll find confidence creeping in little by little. Eventually, when confronted with the test, you'll find yourself responding boldly despite your anxiety.

However, to make your affirmations effective, you need to:

- Do away with random affirmation. It can be very easy to pick up affirmation from anywhere and start saying it. But then, no affirmation resonates like the one you create for yourself. Affirmations created by saying the opposite of the challenges you are going through work more than the ones you pick up from just anywhere.

- Make your affirmations relatable. Whatever you want to say, make sure it relates to you and is achievable. As an athlete, you can say, *"I come out first in the forthcoming race."* But if you are not involved in any race and start saying this to yourself, there's no way it'll resonate with you. Another instance is if you are going for an interview, you can say, *"I can boldly face the interviewer; I'm not afraid of failure because I'm not a failure,"* it relates to your present situation. And for every day, you can create your own affirmation that resonates with you.

- Say them in the present tense. Always keep your affirmations in the present tense, not the future or past tense. For example, *"I have the wisdom to resolve the issues between my friends and me," "I come first in the competition,"* and *"I can face my interviewer boldly and win the job."* The purpose of affirmation is to reorganize your brain into accepting your statements as done, making you react that way. Therefore you shouldn't make those statements in the future or past tense because you want your brain to key into those statements immediately.

- It is not just in the saying. For instance, you can't just wake up and talk about coming out first without competition— the affirmation would be a waste. Similarly, refrain from picking up people's affirmations and lazily uttering them in the morning because somebody told you that affirmation is a good way to start a day. There must be action you want to take; the words are meant to prepare you for those upcoming actions.

- Finally, consistency is key. You say it until you see the change you want to take place effectively. For instance, if you are shy, you want to come out of your shell. You can start affirming boldness in yourself. You keep saying it, even if you end up sheepishly walking out of a conference for the first or second time. Even if you feel you've disappointed yourself by shying away from leadership positions, keep saying the words until the day you find yourself on that podium addressing a small or large crowd. Whatever change you want to effect in your life, you can:

  - Begin by saying the words to yourself at least twice daily, ranging from five to seven minutes.

  - Say it again and again at least ten times.

  - Don't stop saying it until you see yourself become who you want to be.

Continuous daily affirmation ultimately leads to a life you love.

Love Yourself

You'll know you are unique when you see that no one in this world has the same fingerprint as yours. The shape of your face, the curves of your lips and eyebrows, the color of your skin, and the shape of your body—no one can be like you or play your role. Therefore, appreciate yourself, your beauty, and your uniqueness. You are a queen – a goddess – and you can achieve whatever you want. You are unstoppable.

There's nothing as beautiful as the ability to love oneself. So, nothing is as ugly as hating oneself. It is very detrimental and, as a matter of fact, a waste to humanity.

When you love yourself, you'll also care about your physical appearance, mental state, and emotional outlook. When you love yourself, you don't want to be disrespected or trust someone who'll never appreciate you.

When you love yourself, you'll be lovable and attract a love of the same energy. So, when you wake up every morning with your swollen face and messy hair, look at yourself in the mirror and say, *"You are perfectly perfect just the way you are."*

Step Nine
Seek Support and Build a Positive Community

Have you watched the Ben Carson story in the movie *Gifted Hands?* Ben Carson grew up with so much love and care from his mother, who sacrificed so much to see him get an education. However, a part of his teenage years saw a typical good boy suddenly surrounding himself with schoolmates who negatively influenced him.

Ben's association with those friends was the beginning of his exhibiting negative behaviors. He wondered where they came from. He became selfish and self-centered, and he almost once hit his mom with a hammer because he wanted more money than she could give him. Things got worse, and he narrowly escaped killing his friend out of rage. This happened because he had surrounded himself with negative people. Luckily, he decided to rethink this kind of company.

In college, he met Candy, who later became his wife. Candy was such a positive and powerful influence over his life. She believed so much in him that she would always make him see the possibilities in hopeless situations. Whenever he doubted himself, she made him realize he could attain his full potential. Added to the positive influence of Ben's mother, Candy's friendship helped Ben Carson become a successful neurosurgeon.

Having negative people around him only deteriorated Ben's thinking, actions, and relationships. He lost his self-esteem and confidence. Thankfully, he got to retrace his steps to reach his full potential and build a positive community and support system drawn from family and friends around him.

What Being Around Negative People Will Do to Your Mindset

Below is a list of things that can happen to your mindset when you're constantly around negative people.

1. Negative mindset

You become like them when you stick around negative people for too long. There's the famous story of an eaglet hatched in the same nest as some chicks. It never knew what it was for a long time. It went around eating what the chicks ate and behaved just like them. That's exactly what happens when you're always in the company of negative thinkers. You think, act, and end up like them unless you change your circle fast. At times it's not necessarily the company that you keep. It could be a family member, maybe an abusive parent. As they say, "You can choose your friends, but you're stuck with family." No matter how bad it looks, you can get help. You can also take other practical steps to liberate your mind from the damaging effects you've been exposed to over time.

2. Negative and complex emotions

Being around negative people will keep you overwhelmed with negative and complex emotions such as insecurity, anxiety, and depression. Negative people have nothing good to offer you besides pointing out all your faults and flaws. They're specialists in killing any happiness they see in you with their constant negative conversations, teasing, and mocking. With time, you will lose faith in your abilities and feel insecure. You will get anxious about everything and finally fall into depression. This is a dangerous state that has led many teens to think again about being alive.

In this world of free access to the internet, it's very easy for a teen's mindset to be badly affected by negative people online. There have been several cases of teenage girls who committed suicide because of comments left on their social media pages. Such words had badly influenced these girls, and they lost it and gave in to complex and damaging emotions. It would help if you did all you could to protect yourself from an online association that's not beneficial to you.

3. Pessimism

Negative people are typically pessimists. They infect those around them with it. What do pessimists do? They see failure in everything. They have more than enough reasons why things won't work out. So, this is what you'll begin to do when you remain around them. Having pessimists as friends can make your grades drop because you already believe you won't do well even before your exams. It can also affect your relationships because you fear the relationship will not last from the onset. Pessimists don't see any good in sight, only bad things.

4. Fear

This is another trait you exhibit when you're in the company of negative people. Their influence makes you develop a mindset of fear. You are afraid of everything. You're scared you'll be late for school because you already envisage heavy traffic. You're afraid you'll catch a cold just because it's raining. That's such a stressful way to live as a young girl!

5. Lack of motivation

Being around negative people will make you less motivated. That's because their words and actions kill your willpower. They don't encourage your dreams or potential. They make you feel, *You're doing too much already. Why not give it a break?* If you once had goals to achieve, as soon as you start hanging around negative people, you'll think less of working toward achieving them. They don't care about such things as goals. They have nothing besides putting others down, so they think, *Why should you bother?* To attain any height in life, you must avoid negative people.

6. Lack of self-esteem and confidence

Negative people can influence the way you see yourself. They affect the value you place on yourself, however negatively. Since they always highlight your shortcomings, you begin to see things the same way as they do. That can make you lose your confidence and self-worth in the long run. Rather than walk with your head up like you used to, you begin to slouch and look most of the time downward because you are not sure who you are anymore.

7. Trust issues

Negative people will cause you to doubt others and find it hard to maintain good relationships. They'll make you develop an attitude of not trusting people. You will always have a reason to suspect whether people really are who they portray themselves. You may even see others trying to harm you when they want a healthy conversation with you. That can cost you several relationships that should ordinarily improve your life for a long time.

8. Bad behaviors

Staying for a long stretch around negative people will make you lose your good values and pick up destructive behaviors. For example, you can lose respect for your parents because you now think they're not worth holding in high esteem as you've always done. That can make you start talking to them rudely. You may also become disobedient to their rules because you now feel you shouldn't be ordered around by anybody.

It's common for teens to start skipping school after being around negative friends for a while. They will no longer have regard for constituted authority because they think that's the new way to be "cool." Other bad behaviors that can be picked up due to negative people's influence on your mindset are stealing, cheating, lying, and substance abuse.

9. Negative thoughts

Teens can mess up their entire thought pattern by being around negative people. Rather than the productive thoughts you used to have, negative influence can make you think only negative things about yourself and others. That mainly happens when you are alone and trying to reflect on the day's activities. You will begin to remember your negative conversations with the negative persons earlier. Your mind will become saturated with negative thoughts, making you lose peace and joy. It can also affect your health. You may have trouble sleeping because your mind is not relaxed. You wake up and go through the next day mostly uncoordinated.

10. Lack of self-care

Negative people will only make you feel worthless, and you will see no reason to take care of yourself as you should. Because they've made you believe there's nothing good about you, you may eat carelessly, thinking, *Who cares?* In time you will do fewer of those things you used to do to take proper care of yourself.

Seek Support from Family and Friends

The teenage years can be filled with many challenges and changes. It's a time that can determine your success in life. As established earlier, being around negative people will give you a skewed mindset about life, so you should avoid that.

At this point in life, you must draw support from people who can influence you positively.

So, where can you find the needed support? From your family and friends. These are not strangers because you've had a relationship with them for many years. Your family loves you and wants to see you succeed in your endeavors. They are proud when you excel, so they'll do their best to look out for you. The same goes for your true friends—those who think positively and have an optimistic outlook. Such a clique can influence you for the better. With their help, you can attain your heights, improve your confidence, and face your fears.

So, how can you seek support from your family and friends?

1. Be open and honest about your feelings.

It's common to evade questions from parents about sensitive areas of life during the teenage years. That should not be so. Being open and honest with them about your feelings would work best. They can help you only if you make them understand how you feel about certain issues. Then they'll be well-informed enough to guide you. If you think your family is asking you to take a step you're not cool with, you should honestly tell them how you feel rather than get upset and walk away. That is called effective communication. They have communicated their request, and you should express your feelings. By doing this, they can better understand things from your perspective, and you can all come to a compromise.

As a girl, be free to talk with trusted family members when you have friendship issues. Don't shroud everything in secrecy. They can proffer valuable advice and solutions when you're having such problems. You'll also feel safer knowing that they've got your back anytime. Many teens are depressed because they don't open up on sensitive issues. That can easily be avoided when you talk freely and have a support system to fall back on in difficult times.

A lot of girls who have committed suicide as a result of cyber-attacks would still be alive if they were open about their hurt feelings to caring family members and friends. They most likely had hidden their problems from everyone because of the shame or fear of being judged. That is the problem with negative mindsets—you misinterpret things and assume how others will react before they do. Your support group will not judge you even if you deserve to be judged. They'll be more concerned about your welfare than how much you messed up. So, open up and be honest with them as early as possible to avoid losing your sense of proper judgment and taking wrong actions.

2. Ask for help

Don't hesitate to ask for help from friends and family when needed. Don't attempt to do everything on your own. Living in isolation has adverse side effects. Your support group will be happy and willing to help you when in need. *Akeelah and the Bee* is another inspiring movie about a young girl overcoming several challenges to win the Scripps National Spelling Bee competition. Akeelah had to ask for help from family, friends, and neighbors at some point while preparing for the competition. They gladly offered their support in helping her learn new words, and she was able to get adequately prepared for the grand event. While you may think you can do anything, always recognize areas where a little help from others can accelerate your progress.

3. Find time to bond with family and friends

It would help if you found time to bond with your family and friends to feel supported and in circulation. You can do this by spending quality time with them. Don't bury yourself in work or school. Build connections. That will give you a sense of identity outside your career or academics. Find time to share what's happening in your life with them. Call some of them at the end of every day and discuss how your day went. You will find strength from such conversations to keep you going the next day.

4. Talk to trusted adults

Besides family and friends, you can identify other trusted adults from whom you can seek additional support. These include guidance counselors, coaches, teachers, and mentors. You can go to them for professional help and advice when having issues with your academics, relationship, or sports interests. You'll feel better and know the next step after talking to them.

How to Build a Positive Community

Take the following steps to build a positive community to help you interact with people with positive mindsets and attitudes. A positive community can significantly influence you and push you to become all the good things you've ever dreamed of.

1. Volunteering

One good way for teens like you to build a positive community is to volunteer your time, skills, and abilities. Volunteering is an opportunity to meet people who have a positive mindset. School or church projects and those organized by other local groups are avenues to volunteer and meet a positive community.

2. Community Events

Community events like festivals, concerts, and parades are places for positive-minded people to show their support for their community. By participating in such events, you're sure to meet some people you can be good friends with and influence your life positively.

3. Joining a Club

There are various clubs where teens can meet with focused, progressive, and positive people. Such clubs can center on activities like poetry, music, sports, academics, or art. You can carefully look for one that aligns with your interests and become a member. There, you'll be surrounded by people who share the same vision as you. You can easily find encouragement from such groups when you're down or confused about anything. They'll gladly share their experiences with you; in time, you'll find the strength to overcome your challenges. Unlike the negative group that will always tell you "You can't," this group will always let you know "You can."

4. Community Service Projects

Remember, one way to pump up your self-esteem is to help others. Wouldn't it be great to find other people who are also interested in helping others? It's like saying you'll find other people who have self-esteem. I'm sure that would be a great idea! You can find such people when you are involved in community service projects. You can join other people in your spare time to clean the parks, organize food drives, and help at homeless shelters. Not only will it help you feel good about yourself, but you can make a good friend or two.

5. Show of Kindness

You can build a positive community when you show acts of kindness to others. You can do this in little ways, like giving up your seat for a pregnant woman or older adult in a crowded place or opening the door for someone. You can also show kindness by speaking nicely to others and complimenting their outfits. When you come across people you suspect to be new around you, you can be nice to them so they can relax and quickly acclimate to their new location.

Conclusion

Finally, we are at the end of our journey together. Before I go, I have a few words to leave you.

The teenage years are a step toward young adulthood and an opportunity to adjust your self-image, be confident about how you see and carry yourself, and transform your life into a beautiful one.

If you consider the benefits of having high self-esteem and a powerful mindset to create a future you truly want and love, you wouldn't want to give up on that possibility. When you intentionally improve your physical and mental state, you will be confident to play a determinant role in your life. Now that you've learned to build a positive self-image, it's time to stimulate your will and affective qualities to nurture behavioral safety.

Living a happy life is possible, especially when you lay a solid foundation. But how can you live happily ever after if you lack self-love or the mindset to implement your plans? I believe the powerful nine steps in this book could affect your mind positively, and you could begin to take action.

As we bring this book to an end, I hope you don't just close it and forget it. You need to continuously practice if you want to take full control of your life. I know the impact of self-love and how much it can help you grow. Remember not to allow what people think about you to affect who you truly are. Use the steps here to be your compass and guide your journey, and whenever you're confused about what to do next, you can consult the appropriate steps.

Finally, loving yourself first will help you love others. And one way to love people is by giving. So, don't hesitate to help someone change their life just as you have transformed yours. Also, many people suffer from low self-image without seeking help out of shame.

A world where teenagers can live happily, with high self-esteem, and genuinely love themselves is possible! You must have confidence in yourself, relax, and make exploits.

Best wishes.

A RESPECTFUL REQUEST

I hope you enjoyed reading! Please share your story by leaving an **Amazon review**.

Reviews are the lifeblood of any author's career, and for a humbly independent writer like me, every review helps tremendously.

Even if it's only a sentence or two (although the longer the better!), it will be very helpful.

Please scan the below QR code to leave your review now.

Alternatively, you can visit:
www.bit.ly/review-self-love

Thank you.

A FREE GIFT TO OUR READERS

For being our valued reader, we are offering you 3 books absolutely FREE today.

What You'll Get:

✔ **11 Essential Life Skills** Every Teen Needs to Learn Before Leaving Home

✔ How to **Be A Calm Parent** Even When Your Teens Drive You Crazy

✔ 15 Tips to **Build Self-Esteem and Confidence** in Teen Boys & Girls

Scan the below QR code to download now.

Alternatively, you can visit:
www.thementorbucket.com/gift-self-love

MORE RECOMMENDED BOOKS

SELF-ESTEEM FOR TEENS

Mastering Self-Love and Building Limitless Confidence
(A Proven Path to Transform Your Life and
Achieve Your Dreams)

Get more details here:

www.thementorbucket.com/self-esteem

LIFE SKILLS
FOR TEENS WORKBOOK

35+ Essentials for Winning in the Real World
(How to Cook, Manage Money, Drive a Car, and
Develop Manners, Social Skills, and More)

Get more details here:

www.thementorbucket.com/life-skills-teens

WANT TO READ MORE?

Before I close, I recommend you to read our other books in the series. These books are written especially for teens and their parents. You'll find them very helpful.

Get more details here:

www.thementorbucket.com/resources

Made in the USA
Las Vegas, NV
21 March 2024

87501128R00083